Your Decisions Determine Your Destiny

By Ralph Phifer

All scripture references are taken from the King James Version of the Holy Bible, unless otherwise stated.

YOUR DECISIONS DETERMINE YOUR DESTINY

Revised Edition

DEDICATION

I dedicate this book to my darling wife, Bridget, for her support and encouragement. To my loving mother, Shirley A. Phifer who has inspired me to be what God created me to be. To Wendy Brown and Linda Alomia whose hunger and thirst after the Lord has inspired me to desire a greater anointing. Blessed are they that hunger and thirst after righteousness, for they shall be filled.

ACKNOWLEDGEMENTS

No one person can take the credit for accomplishing something. You are what you are by the grace of God. No man is an island. You are a product of the people who have influenced your life - people, who taught you, loved you, and put time, effort, or money into you. They told you when you were right and when you were wrong. They cried with you, and laughed with you. The same is no different in the writing of this book. I would like to thank some very special people who contributed to this book: Bridget Phifer, Jana Dale, LaVerne Caffey, Little David, and John Clingenpeel. Thank you, and may God give you a hundred-fold return.

Contents

Chapter

Introduction

As I was sitting on my mother's sofa one day watching TV, the Lord spoke to me and said, "You are what you are based on the decisions that you make." Not being sure of what I heard I said, "What?" Once again the Lord spoke and said, "You are what you are based on the decisions you make." I began to meditate and ponder what was said to me. The more I pondered on that statement the more I saw the truth of that statement. God gave us the ability to make our own decisions in life. He gave Adam and Eve the right to choose. God is saying that your success or failure in life is a result of your ability to make choices.

God has a plan and a purpose for your life. In order to fulfill your destiny, you must learn to make wise decisions. Many people in life are not doing what God called them to do because they are making bad decisions. All of us at one point in time have made bad decisions, and those decisions may have cost us a great deal. But that doesn't mean we can't put those decisions behind us, learn from them, and move on.

Some people have made bad financial decisions, bad marriage decisions, or bad friendship decisions. Some have chosen not to follow God, and it cost them dearly. Some people have chosen not to accept Jesus as Lord and Savior, and will pay the ultimate price for that bad decision, and that is an eternity in hell.

Decisions, decisions, decisions. Each and every day of our lives we are faced with decisions. Some are not as big as others. Some are not as important as others. But it is very important that we all improve our decision-making skills.

I was so impacted by the statement, "You are what you are based on the decisions you make," that I decided to write this book. I hope to give you some insights on how important the decisions that we make are. The decisions we make in life determine our destiny. I also hope to illustrate to you how to make good quality and godly decisions. May this book be a blessing to you, because your decisions will determine your destiny!

Chapter 1

The Choice is Yours

The single most powerful thing that we as people possess is *the power of choice*. Success or failure is based on the decisions we make in life. So many people are blaming God, the devil, the white man, the black man, where they came from, and anything else they can think of for their circumstance. But I am here to tell you that you are what you are, based on the decisions that you make! The late Dr. Lester Sumrall said, "Man makes a decision, and the decision makes the man."

God made us free moral agents, meaning we have the right to make our own decisions. The devil can't *make* us do anything. He can only tempt us. You and I have the ability to resist him, if we are under the Blood of Jesus. The Lord God commanded the man saying:

"Of every tree of the garden thou mayest freely eat; But, of the tree of knowledge of good and evil, thou shalt not eat; For in the day thou eatest, thou shalt surely die."

Genesis 2:16, 17

God gave Adam and Eve a choice. He put neither guard dogs around the tree of life, nor a barbed wire fence. He simply told them not to eat of the tree of knowledge of good and evil. He informed them of the consequences they would experience if they were to disobey His command. When the serpent came to tempt them, they were faced with a decision - either they were going to do what God said, or give in to the devil. Unfortunately, they chose to obey the devil rather than God. Yet after exercising their power of choice, they did not want to accept the consequences. Once God confronted them, they wanted to play the blame game. Adam blamed God for giving him the woman. Eve blamed the serpent that in turn probably looked around to see if he could place the blame somewhere else! This is so typical of us; wanting to blame other people, or circumstances, for our plight in life. It is time we took responsibility for our own actions. God was not to blame, and neither was the serpent. Adam and Eve made the decision themselves to eat the forbidden fruit. Therefore, they were to blame. Adam more so than Eve, because he was the man and God had made him the head. He should have stood up and said, "We are not going to eat this fruit because God said not to eat of this tree."

"And if it seems evil unto you to serve the Lord, choose you this day whom ye will serve; whether the gods which your fathers served that were on the other side of the floods, or the gods of the Amorites in whose land ye dwell: But, as for me and my house, we will serve the Lord."

Joshua 24:15

Joshua told the people that they had a choice to make. Either they were going to serve the *true and the living God,* or they could bow down to false gods. He then stated: *"But as for me and my house, we will serve the Lord."* Joshua took a stand and made the decision for his family. He did not say, "Honey, do you and the kids think we ought to serve the Lord?" No, unlike Adam, Joshua stood up as the Priest of the home, and stated how they were going to serve the Lord. We need men today who will stand up and confirm that they and their families will serve the Lord.

Some people think that it is not fair that they should suffer because of what Adam and Eve did. My friend, *you don't have to suffer!* You have the power of choice, just as they did. Either you are going to obey God, or you will conform to the devil's plans and ideas.

I call heaven and earth to record this day against you, that I have set before you life and death, blessing and cursing: therefore choose life, that both thou and thy seed may live.

Deuteronomy 30:19

God gave the children of Israel a choice. Not only did He give them a choice, but He also told them what choice they ought to make - He said, "Choose life." God could not make the choice for them, because He gave them the right to make their own decisions. Not only was God talking to the children of Israel then, but He is also talking to you and I today. He is telling us that we have decisions to make, and He is guiding us in the direction we should go, because our decisions determine our destiny.

All through the Bible, men and women were faced with decisions. Consider Pilate - he had the decision to release Jesus or Barabas. He chose Barabas over Jesus. Joseph chose not to sleep with Potiphar's wife. Daniel and the three Hebrew boys chose not to bow to false gods. Judas chose to betray Jesus, for thirty pieces of silver. Cain made the decision to kill Abel his brother. Ananias and Sapphira chose to lie to the Holy Ghost. Noah decided to build the ark, even though it had never rained before. Reflect upon the decision Jesus made to leave

Heaven and to come to earth, to die for you and me. God has given us the ability to make our own decisions. It is up to us to make the right choice.

Adam's Choice

And the Lord God commanded the man saying, Of every tree of the garden thou mayest freely eat: But of the tree of the knowledge of good and evil, thou shalt not eat of it: for in the day that thou eatest thereof thou shalt surely die.

Genesis 2:16, 17

God gave Adam a choice, and He gave him the consequences of that choice. He told him that he would surely die if he ate of the tree. Now we see that God was not talking about a physical death, because when he ate of the tree he did not fall dead. But He meant he would die spiritually, which means he would be separated from God. And eventually, he would die physically. There is something I noticed that is very interesting to me. God did not say, "And in addition to you dying, all mankind will also suffer..." Yet that is exactly what happened. Because of Adam's decision, you and I were born sinners. *We* did not disobey God. So why do *we* have to pay for a decision that someone else made? One might ask the question, "Why am I put in a situation where I have to make a decision that will determine where I spend eternity because of one man who disobeyed God - is that fair?"

For as by one man's disobedience many were made sinners, so by the obedience of one shall many be made righteous.

Romans 5:19

Even though Adam blew it, God had a replacement, and that replacement is the Lord Jesus Christ. Even though we didn't eat the fruit, we also didn't die at Calvary. God is a just God. God is a fair God. God has put us in the same situation Adam was in. We all have a choice to make. What if it were you in the garden? Would you have made the right decision?

I once heard a story of a plantation worker who was working in the fields. One day, as he worked, he would yell, "Oh Adam, oh Adam." The plantation owner asked him, "Why are you yelling, 'Oh Adam, oh Adam'?" And the worker said, "If it wasn't for Adam I would not have to be out here working so hard in these fields." The owner thought for a moment and said, "I'll make you a deal. I am going to let you live in the house; you have access to anything you want - food, transportation, and living quarters - anything you want. But, there is one condition. The big white vase in the living room, whatever you do, don't look under it. If you do you will have to return to the fields and never complain again." The worker agreed. The owner was out of town for a week. The worker was living the best life he had ever lived - eating the finest foods, sleeping in the finest beds, the best transportation. But, every time he walked past the vase, he couldn't help but wonder what was under that vase. One day as he looked at the vase he said, "There's no way he can tell if I looked under it," and his curiosity got the best of him. So he slowly raised the vase, and out quickly shot a white mouse. He tried to catch the mouse, but to no avail. When the owner returned and the mouse was gone, he turned to the worker and said, "What do you think about Adam now?" The point I am trying to make is that we all have made wrong decisions. It's so easy for us to say, "I wouldn't have done that," but put in that same situation, you don't know what you would do. You and I *are* in the situation that Adam was in; we have a choice to make.

We can learn from others' mistakes and make a wise decision.

Decisions Have Consequences

Behold, I set before you this day a blessing and a curse: A blessing, if ye obey the commandments of the word of God, which I command you this day: A curse, if ye will not obey the commandments of the word of God, but turn aside out of the way in which I command you this day: to go after other gods which ye have not known.
Deuteronomy 11:26, 27, 28

Every decision that we make has a consequence. When God gives a commandment He expects us to follow it. If we do not, then there may be natural and spiritual consequences we will have to accept. Thank God for His grace and mercy, but too many people make the mistake of thinking that forgiveness eliminates consequences. An example of this is the woman caught in adultery. The people brought her to Jesus, and said the law stated that she must be stoned to death. Jesus replied saying, "He without sin, cast the first stone." The people turned away, of course, because none of them was without sin. Jesus then told the woman to go and sin no more. We seem to want to think that everything was over then. What about the other people involved - were there consequences? The woman was <u>caught</u> in adultery, which constitutes that one or both of them were married. What about the other spouse? How do you think they felt? What if she had kids? They would have to go around being teased and made fun of because of what their mother had done. What about her husband? The embarrassment he would have to face. Would he want a divorce from her? Sure those people went away that day, but she still had to face them once Jesus left. The whispers she would hear. I have no evidence that any of these things happened. I am simply trying to show you that just because you are forgiven, it does not necessarily mean that there will be no consequences to face.

When David committed adultery with Bathsheba, and had her husband killed by sending him on the front line at war, David had to pay for what he did. God forgave him, but he still had to pay a price for his sin. The baby died that had been conceived as a result of their adultery. And after almost a year going by without David dealing with the situation, God sent Nathan the prophet to reveal to him what was going to happen. God was giving David room to repent, but David didn't deal with the issue. After Nathan told David a parallel story, David announced the judgment of the man in the narrative, not knowing he was pronouncing his own judgment. When David realized what he had done, he fell on his knees and asked the Lord to forgive him. God forgave him, but that does not negate the fact that David had to pay for his sin. David's children were violent and murderous. His own children rose up against him. They tried to overthrow his throne and kill him. Yes, the Lord forgave David, but the seeds he planted came to harvest.

I know many people who have made bad decisions concerning marriage partners. The first little thing that goes wrong, they want to get a divorce. You must realize that you made a decision to marry that person. Don't try to use the excuse that God wants you to get a divorce and then marry someone else. God was probably giving you signs all along telling you not to marry that person in the first place, and you just ignored the signs. I would not suggest to anyone to get a divorce. However, I am not insinuating that anyone should stay with a person if they are being physically or mentally abused, or their life might be in danger. A divorce, however, is not always the right solution. The first step should be to get away from the abusive relationship, and seek spiritual and natural advice, and counseling. Many churches provide counseling and assistance for this type of situation.

The point I am trying to make is that decisions have consequences. Before making a decision we need to recognize the consequences that may follow. If I rob a bank and get caught, I can ask God to forgive me, and He will. However, this does not mean that I won't go to jail. This is because the law states that if you rob a bank, you will be punished and sentenced to jail. If we make the decision to rob the bank in the first place, we should be willing to face the consequences. I have heard so many people say, "Why did God let me get caught?" It is not God's fault that you chose to make a bad decision even though you knew the consequences.

I have talked about the negative results of disobedience; now let's talk about the fruits of obedience. For instance, the three Hebrew boys refused to bow to Nebuchadnezzar's statue. They knew they would be tossed into the fiery furnace, but they stood on the Word of God, believing that God was true to His Word. They believed that God would deliver them out of the furnace, and God did deliver them. Noah obeyed God and built an ark, despite the fact that it had never rained. Noah followed God's direction, and he was able to save his family from the destructive floods. Daniel refused to stop praying to God, and was delivered out of the lion's den. Abraham obeyed God, and is called the father of our faith. He lived a prosperous life and raised godly seed. Moses obeyed God, and led the children of Israel out of Egypt. The point here is that there are fruits for obedience as well as disobedience.

Consequences Are Not Always Manifested Immediately

When we plant a seed, that seed does not produce a crop over night.

Sometimes, when we make a decision, the results of that decision are not manifested right away. For example if you have planted a seed of smoking, it may be years before that seed starts to produce a crop. That crop could be cancer, emphysema, heart disease, lung disease, etc. If you choose to have sex outside of marriage, you may not see the result of that seed until months later. The result may be a child, a sexually transmitted disease, or a soul tie to that person you had sex with. Some people seem to think that because they have not yet been caught or punished, they are getting away with their sin. Not so; it may be that their crop has not yet produced, or God may be giving them room to repent. I remember Brother Kenneth E. Hagin telling a story of a man who wanted Brother Hagin to pray for his healing. The Lord spoke to him and told him the man was going to die, and that He had given this man 30 years to repent. It could be that God is giving you room to repent. Someone might say, "Well then, I too will have 30 years to get it right." Not so! That was that man's measure of mercy and judgment, not yours! God deals differently with different people and different situations.

"Be not deceived, God is not mocked: for whatsoever a man soweth, that shall he also reap. For he that soweth to the flesh shall of the flesh reap corruption. But, he that soweth to the spirit shall of the spirit reap life everlasting."
Galatians 6:7, 8

Just as it takes time for bad seeds to produce, it also takes time for good seeds to produce. Just because you tithe today doesn't mean you are going to reap a million dollars next week. You have to be steadfast and persistent.

"And let us be not weary in well doing: for in due season we shall reap, if we faint not."
Galatians 6:9

It doesn't happen like instant grits; it takes time. You may be praying for an unsaved loved one and they may seem to be getting worse, but keep praying and thanking God for sending laborers across their paths. I was in a service one time, and a man came down and gave his life to Christ. The pastor knew that the father of the man had been praying for this day. The father came down with tears in his eyes, and said that he had been praying for his son for 27 years. I said, "Wow, 27 years!" We are supposed to be steadfast and persevering, yet if our prayers aren't answered next week, we start complaining and questioning God, "What's wrong?" Twenty-seven years that man prayed and believed every day for his son. He encouraged us not to stop believing God, no matter what the situation seems like. What I am saying is, whether they are good or bad, it takes time for the consequences to manifest. Hold on to the Word of God. Build your faith. Renew your mind to the things of God.

"Being confident of this very thing, that He which hath begun a good work in you will perform it until the day of Jesus Christ."
Philippians 1:6

Hang in there and keep persevering. Keep your eyes on the prize. Just like the farmer that plants his crop - he has to water it, and keep the birds and insects off of it. He has to till the ground, and make sure it has good soil to grow in. He goes to bed and gets up, then goes to bed and gets up again. But when the harvest is finally come, it is worth all the work he has put into it. Know that your harvest is coming; **be not weary in well doing**.

Chapter 2

A Destiny Decision

When I talk about decisions, I am talking about destiny decisions. I am not talking about whether or not you should go to McDonalds or Burger King for lunch. I am talking about decisions that will determine whether or not you will fulfill your God-given destiny. Ministries fail because of bad decisions; marriages file for divorce because of bad decisions; Fortune 500 companies file for bankruptcy because of bad decisions. On the other hand, ministries flourish because of good decisions; marriages are successful because of good decisions; companies become Fortune 500 companies because of good decisions.

What is a destiny decision? A destiny decision is Samson not being able to keep his head out of Delilah's lap, or Joseph being able to flee from Potiphar's wife. A destiny decision is Daniel and the three Hebrew boys purposing in their heart that they would not defile themselves neither with the king's meat, nor with the wine which he drank. A destiny decision is Ruth and her sister Orpah being faced with a decision to stay in Moab or go to Bethlehem with Naomi. Orpah chose to stay, while Ruth told Naomi, "Where you go I will go, your God will be my God." As a result, she ended up marrying billionaire Boaz and was incorporated into the genealogy of Jesus. A

14

destiny decision is Moses refusing to be called the son of pharaoh's daughter, choosing rather to suffer affliction with the people of God, than to enjoy the pleasures of sin for a season. A destiny decision is Elisha leaving everything to follow Elijah, knowing his destiny was at stake. A destiny decision is Abraham leaving his home to go to a place he knew not of, because God told him to. I believe at certain points and times in your life you will be faced with some destiny decisions. I pray you make the right choice.

You Are What You Have Become

You are what you have become. That's a powerful statement. Just think about it – *you are what you have become!* My friend, each and every day of your life you are becoming something. Dr. Myles Munroe said that we are the sum total of everything we have learned. You become what you think about. The Bible says, **"For as he (a man) thinketh in his heart so is he." (Proverbs 23:7)**.

You become what you meditate on. The Bible says you should **meditate on the Word day and night (Joshua 1:8)**. You become what you constantly hear. Jesus said, **"He who has ears to hear, let him hear." (Matthew 11:15)**

You are a product of the books you read, the environment you expose yourself to, the sermons you hear, the seminars you attend, the people you fellowship with, the words you speak, and the words you believe. When you look at different areas of your life, whether the spiritual, physical, financial, vocational, intellectual, or relational, wherever you are in those areas of your life, it is due to the fact that you have become what you are.

I believe you have become what you are because of the decisions you have made. Everyday of our lives we are faced with decisions within these areas, and our decisions will determine how our life turns out. I heard that one of the greatest qualities on earth is the willingness to become. You are what you have become, but the good thing about that is you have a lot to say about what you become. The decisions *you* make will decide what you will become.

Thinking Determines Decisions

The way you think will determine the way you live. I say that because every action begins with a thought. If you reach to scratch your nose, you had to think about it first, even though it may seem like a natural reaction.

For as he thinketh in his heart, so is he...

Proverbs 23:7

The Bible says you become what you think about. Listen to this statement I heard once: "Man is not what he thinks he is, but what he *thinks,* he *is!*" Now read it again very slowly, and put the emphasis on the verbs in the second part. "...But what he *thinks* (emphasis, pause), he *is* (emphasis*)."*

And be not conformed to this world: but be ye transformed by the renewing of your mind, that ye may prove what is that good, and acceptable, and perfect will of God.

Romans 12:2

I believe the most important thing that a person must do after accepting Jesus Christ as their Lord and Savior is renew their mind with the Word of God. Why does Romans 12:2 tell us to do that? It tells us to do that because if we don't, we will continue to act the same way we did before we got saved. That's because thinking determines decisions. This is why it's very important that we control our thinking. In Philippians 2:5, it says to let this mind be in you that was also in Christ Jesus. As Christians we should have the mind of Christ, so that we can display the actions of Christ. Romans 12:2 states that your mind needs to be renewed so you may prove what is that which is good, acceptable and perfect will of God. However, you can't do the will of God until you renew your mind with the Word of God.

But if our gospel be hid, it is hid to them that are lost: in whom the God of this world hath blinded the minds of them which believe not, lest the light of the glorious gospel of Christ, who is the image of God, should shine unto them.

2 Corinthians 4:3, 4

The devil knows that thinking determines decisions. The Bible says that if our gospel be hid, it is hid to them that are lost, in whom the God of this world (satan), hath blinded the minds of them which believe not. The devil wants to hide the gospel from you and me. Why? Because if we hear the gospel, and believe the gospel, then we will act on the gospel. He blinds the minds of them which believe not. He wants to control your thoughts. He will try to fill your mind with thoughts that are contrary to the Word of God. If he can control your mind, he can control your life. In the Old Testament the pharaoh knew the power of thinking. In essence, he was saying, "The children of Israel are much greater in number than we are. We must afflict them, so that mentally they will believe that we are still in control. Even though they could possibly overtake us, they will not attempt it because mentally they don't believe they can." Your thinking will determine the decisions you make.

Three Ways Your Thinking Is Developed:

1. HEARING

Jesus said that he who has ears to hear, should hear what the word of the Lord says. One way your thinking is developed is by hearing.

For whosoever shall call upon the name of the Lord shall be saved. How then shall they call Him in whom the have not believed? And how shall they believe in Him of whom they have not heard? And how shall they hear without a preacher?

Romans 10:13, 14

The scripture says before you can believe you must first hear. You first of all hear something. From there you determine whether or not you are going to believe what you heard. Then the way you think about what you heard determines how you respond to it. Hearing determines thinking. Thinking determines decisions.

So then faith cometh by hearing, and hearing by the Word of God.

Romans 10: 17

To have faith you must first of all hear. Then you think about what you heard. Then you determine

18

whether or not you are going to believe what you heard.

Then you act. Hearing affects thinking.

2. <u>SEEING</u>
For we walk by faith, not by sight.

2 Corinthians 5:7

It's interesting what this scripture says. It doesn't say for we walk by faith, not by what we hear. Nor does it say we walk by faith, not by what we feel. It says sight because our natural sight is one of the most powerful senses we have. It's telling us that we can't depend on what we see with our natural eyes. This is because what we see can be very persuasive. Look at what 2 Corinthians 4:18 says – "While we look not at the things which are seen, but at the things which are not seen". It's saying, that we should not look at the things we see happening around us, because those things can be very deceptive. It says those things we see with the natural eye are subject to change. We must look at things with our spiritual eyes. If we don't, those things we see with our natural eyes can overwhelm us.

My son, attend to my words; incline thine ear unto my sayings. Let them not depart from thine eyes; keep them in the midst of thine heart.

First of all, it says incline thine ear unto my sayings. In other words, listen very closely. Next, it says do not let them depart from thine eyes. Why? Because what you hear and what you see will determine how you think, and how you think will determine your decisions.

3. WHAT YOU EXPERIENCE
Recently I was talking to a woman who had experienced a very bad marriage. She talked about how she no longer trusted men. She went on, and on, about how men are no good and how they just want to use you, and throw you away, and so on. You see, she didn't think very highly of men. The reason she didn't think highly of men was because of her experience with her ex-husband. The things you experience in life will have a great effect on how you think about certain things. I think about the disciples and when they followed Jesus - they experienced many things. The things they experienced had to have a great effect on their thinking - the miracles that He performed; the healings that they experienced themselves.

We were all raised in different environments and cultures, some good, some bad. We all have different influences in our lives; teachers, coaches, friends, relatives, co-workers, etc. And because of this, we experienced different things. People have had bad experiences concerning churches and preachers, and because of their experiences, they no longer trust in God.

The children of Israel are a classic example. They were in slavery for 430 years. God sent Moses to deliver them out of the hands of Pharaoh. They were delivered out of the hands of Pharaoh. But because of the experiences they had encountered, their thinking never changed. Even though God performed miracle after miracle, they could not shake that slave mentality. They always referred back to when they were in Egypt. Except for their children, they ended up dying in the wilderness, never reaching the land of milk and honey that God had for them. They allowed the experiences in Egypt to rob them of God's destiny for their lives. So many people today are missing out on God's plan for their lives because they cannot get past the things they have experienced or are experiencing.

Chapter 3

Our Decisions Affect Others

We seem to think that our decisions only affect us. You have heard people say, "What I do is my business, it's my life; I won't be hurting anyone but myself." Wrong! Your decisions not only affect your life, but they affect the lives of others.

In an earlier chapter I talked about Adam's decision affecting all mankind. Because of Adam's decision, everyone is born with a sin nature. Jesus is called the second Adam. Jesus also made a decision that affected all mankind. Suppose Jesus had not made the decision to come to earth to give His life as a ransom for you and me. We would all be in big trouble.

David made a decision that also affected others. In 2 Samuel 24, we read that David's heart began to grow with pride. He numbered Israel and Judah. Taking a census was not wrong, because God had previously ordered Moses to take two censuses. However, God did not want David to think his success was based on the number of people he had fighting for him. After David had numbered the people, his heart convicted him, and he repented for what he had done. His deed did not go unpunished. The Lord offered David three things he could choose from for punishment: 1.) Seven years of famine would come to the land; 2.) David would flee three months from his enemy while they pursued him, and 3.) There would be three days of pestilence in the land. David chose to let the Lord decide the punishment. The Lord chose the three days of pestilence for his punishment. As a result of the pestilence, 70,000 men died. David made a decision that cost 70,000 men their lives. *Our decisions don't only affect us; they affect others as well.*

When a drunk driver kills someone, his decision to drink and drive does not only affect him. What about the person he killed? What about the family and friends of the person killed? What about the drunk driver's family? What about the boss who has lost a worker? *Our decisions not only affect us; they affect others as well.*

God has a call on your life. He has ordained you to minister to certain people, to take the gospel to certain people. Your gifts, talents, and abilities are needed to change people's lives. Your decision to do what God has called you to do is affecting other people's lives. Someone is waiting for you. You have the answer they have been looking for. You see, even when you don't decide, you have already decided. I don't want to have someone waiting on me for his or her answer. How about you?

The Curse is Broken

Many people today are walking around defeated because of generational curses within their families. An example of a generation curse is one that is passed down from your great-great-grandfather, to your great-grandfather, to your grandfather, to your father, to you.

"Thou shalt not bow down thyself to them, nor serve them; for I the Lord thy God am a jealous God, visiting the iniquity of the fathers upon the children unto the third and forth generation of them that hate me."
Exodus 20:5

As I said in the previous chapter, the decisions we make not only affect us, but they affect others as well. When people tell us that "it is my life," that they can do what they want to do, that they are not hurting anyone but themselves, my friend, they are sadly mistaken. God tells us that the sins of the father will be passed down to the children, unto the third and fourth generations. Why do you think a child that grows up in an alcoholic family, that goes through all sorts of pain and heartbreak, would then themself become an alcoholic? They repeat the same actions of their parents. Why would a person that was abused as a child grow up and abuse others and their own family members? Or, you may have witnessed your parents go through a divorce, and then find yourself as an adult going through a divorce as well. These are some examples of curses that have been passed down from generation to generation. The curse of poverty, stealing, lying, perversions, pornography, depression, drugs, rebellious children, wife-beating, witchcraft, disease, or sickness are all generational curses, to name a few. If a curse you are enduring was not mentioned above, just fill in the blank. Whatever the curse, it may have been passed down through the generations of your family. A woman may find herself trying to dominate her husband, and yet she doesn't understand why. She may be acting like her mother, her grandmother, or great-grandmother. The woman may not want to act like this, but because of a generation curse, she is unable to resist this type of behavior.

Sin causes pain. In Genesis 3:16 and 17, God told Adam and Eve the consequences of their sin. Not only did it affect them, but it also affected the whole world.

"Wherefore by one man sin entered into the world and death by sin; and so death passed upon all men for that all have sinned."

Romans 5:12

We are born sinners by nature. If you notice we don't have to teach a child to lie, or we don't have to teach a child to be selfish. It seems more natural for them to lie than to tell the truth. We must teach a child to tell the truth because lying comes naturally.

"For the wages of sin is death: But the gift of God is eternal life through Jesus Christ our Lord."

Romans 6:23

The beautiful thing about God is that He always gives us a way of escape. The wages of sin is death, *BUT THE GIFT OF GOD IS ETERNAL LIFE THROUGH JESUS CHRIST OUR LORD!* The *GOOD NEWS* is that we no longer have to live under generational curses.

"In those days, they shall say no more, The fathers have eaten a sour grape, and the children's teeth are set on edge. But, everyone shall die for his own iniquity; every man that eateth the sour grape, his teeth shall be set on edge."

Jeremiah 31:29, 30

We now see that we have a choice in being accountable for our father's sins. The blood of Jesus broke the curse. When we accept Jesus as our Lord and Savior, whatever curses our families may have endured in the past are broken. A person can no longer say that he or she is an alcoholic just because their father or mother was one. The person is an alcoholic because they choose to be one.

Once again we are faced with a decision. Christ became a curse for us. We may suffer now from a generational curse, but it does not have to remain that way. God has provided us with an escape, which is the blood of Jesus Christ. The *CHOICE* is yours!

Feeling Obligated

I want to be very careful as I write this section. I want you to pay very close attention. We have certain obligations in life, and we should make decisions based on obligations. However, sometimes people make bad decisions because they "feel" obligated. Let me give you an example. God told Abraham to leave his father and mother, and go to a land that He would show him. Abraham took Lot, his nephew, but God did not tell Abraham to take Lot. Abraham, "feeling" that it was his obligation, took Lot anyhow. He probably felt it was his responsibility to take care of Lot. We all know Lot caused Abraham great heartaches and problems.

Sometimes we "feel" like we are obligated to do something, when in reality we are not. I know of a pastor's wife who had a nervous breakdown, because she "felt" she had to do everything everyone wanted her to do, all because she was a pastor's wife. If she couldn't be at church for every event, she felt guilty, even though she may have had something important to do. For example, one of her children may have been sick, but she would still try to make an event. Although she felt obligated to the church, taking care of her child was much more important than the church event.

Many pastors burn out because they have to visit every person, and their uncle, in the hospital. They "feel" they have to take care of every situation that arises. If Sister Sally's cat dies, they "feel" they have to visit. They "feel" guilty if they take a vacation. If they do take a vacation, they don't enjoy it because they are so concerned about what is going on at the church. I know of a nationally known pastor who pastors a congregation of about 15,000, who had a nervous breakdown. It was said that he had not taken a vacation in at least ten years. He "felt" he *had* to be there to oversee every situation. Yes, he had obligations, but we are not obligated to oversee everything all of the time.

I have a friend who fathered a child out of wedlock before he got saved. Once he was saved, he "felt" it was his obligation to marry the mother of his child. The woman was not saved. The two had dated prior to him getting saved, but they were no longer together. They were headed in two different directions, but he felt that because they had a child together he should marry her. They got married and had major problems, mostly due to the fact that he was serving God and she wasn't. They were separated a few times and have talked about divorce. He told me the reason he married her was because he felt obligated to *her,* not because he loved her, or wanted to be with her. *He was obligated to take care of his child*, not to marry her because they had a child. He made a decision because he felt obligated. The decision was not a wise one. It is never a good decision when the decision is based on a false sense of obligation.

A famous gospel singer told how she married a man because the arrangements were already made, and people were there, family had flown in, the works. She had a bad feeling about walking down the aisle, but she felt obligated because the work was already done. Money was spent and the guests were waiting. That man physically abused her and could possibly have killed her. She failed to heed the check in her spirit, and because she felt obligated to the people who had worked so hard and had come to the wedding, she made a bad decision.

I know of another situation where a friend of mine tried to take care of a family member because she felt obligated. My friend's aunt was having problems, and was not able to care for her son. The young boy went from household to household within the family. It got to a point where the rest of the family felt it would be best to put her son in foster care, but because he was a relative of hers, my friend felt obligated to take him in. She was already a single parent, with too many other responsibilities. Finally it was too much for her to handle, and she had to turn the young boy over to someone outside of her family to care for him. She had made a decision to care for the boy because she felt obligated.

Sometimes we feel that because of relatives and friends we are obligated to fix everything. Although we do have obligations in many areas of our lives, and we need to deal with our obligations accordingly, it is never good to make a decision just because you *feel obligated;* we must weigh the full matter. There are times when we receive a false sense of obligation. I am trying to say that, yes, we have obligations, but we must be wise, and not make decisions solely based on feeling obligated, when in reality we are not.

Chapter 4

Decisions Require Faith

"**By faith, Moses when he was come to years, refused to be called the son of the Pharaoh's daughter: choosing rather to suffer affliction with the people of God than enjoy the pleasures of sin for a season. Esteeming the reproach of Christ greater riches than the treasures in Egypt, for he had respect unto the recompense of the reward. By faith he forsook Egypt, not fearing the wrath of the king; for he had endured, as seeing Him who is invisible.**"

Hebrews 11:24-27

God will not ask you to do anything that doesn't require faith. My decision based on the Word of God will require faith. The Bible says, "We walk by faith, not by sight." Moses made a decision based on his relationship with God. His choice was not based on what his physical senses saw. Moses was thinking about eternity rather than this physical world. Moses could have had all the riches, women, and possibly a succession to Pharaoh's throne. Most people would have taken the materialistic position without hesitation or a second thought. Moses knew that the physical and material possessions were only temporal, but the things of God are eternal.

The world measures a person's success on the amount of material possession they gain. Moses esteemed

Christ to be greater than the riches of Pharaoh. If Moses had accepted the role Pharaoh's daughter had prepared for him, he could have lived in that wealth for 80 years, (he lived to be 120 years old and Moses was 40 when God placed him on the backside of the desert). But Moses chose rather to follow and obey God, whose reward was for an eternity.

Sin may appear to be fun, but it only lasts for a season, for just a little while. Don't let others fool you into thinking sin is not fun. The Bible uses the term *pleasures of sin;* supporting that sin *is* fun. Having an affair probably seems like fun, until a person gets caught. Smoking starts out as fun, until the person discovers they have lung cancer. Drinking can be a lot of fun, until a person finds out they have permanent liver damage. Sex outside of marriage is perceived as fun, until a person is diagnosed with A.I.D.S., or a woman finds out she is pregnant. Cheating on your income taxes may seem like fun, until the IRS catches the person. Cheating on a test in school may seem fun, until the person is caught and expelled. Sin may be fun all right; but it is only for a season.

"For the wages of sin is death: but the gift of God is eternal life through Jesus Christ our Lord."
Romans 6:23

Moses has been dead for close to 3000 years. He is in heaven with God enjoying the benefits of his decision. Moses could have lived it up in the Pharaoh's house, but chose rather to obey God. He has gone down in history as one of the greatest men of God. Moses based his decision on the things of God as opposed to the things of the world.

Abraham is called the father of faith. In Genesis 12:1, we see God calling Abram, not yet named Abraham, to leave his country and his father's house. God tells Abraham that he will make him a great nation. God said to Abram that He would bless him and that he would be a blessing. Abram believed God and departed from his country. Abram's actions required faith. When we study this further, we realize Abram was comfortable in his own country, and very settled in his own homeland. Things were going well for Abram. All of a sudden, God instructs Abram to leave his home and follow God. My friend, this takes an extremely strong faith.

"But without faith it is impossible to please Him, for He that cometh to God must believe..."
Hebrews 11:6

For he that comes to God must believe that He is, and that He is a rewarder of them that diligently seek Him. In order to please God, you must have faith. Many people have to see the whole picture before they will act on God's word. If you are one of these people, you will limit the hand of God moving in your life.

Faith is a firm persuasion based on confident expectation. Abraham was fully persuaded that God was able to do all that He said He would do. We must take God at His word. Abraham acted on what God said to him before he saw the actual manifestation of God's promises. Abraham hoped in God's word. He had a confident expectation. He was confident that God was able to do all that He promised. We have to stand on God's word regardless of what we might see, or feel, or hear. Many people have been robbed of the blessings that God has already provided for them because they are unable to hope in His word. They are unable to stand on God's word to them. We must realize just because healing may not be manifested the moment we pray, it doesn't mean God's word doesn't work. *God's word works!* We must hold onto His word and continue to thank God for manifesting His word. Sometimes that seed of the word needs to be watered and protected, covered in scriptures, and covered with your confession. It needs to be spoken to, nourished, and protected from the birds in order for it to grow.

Faith, too, must be developed over time. The word of God works if you work the word. I am sure that Abraham's family members tried to talk him out of leaving home. However, Abraham was sold on obeying God. People may try to talk you out of your blessing, and not necessarily unbelievers, even Spirit-filled Christians. The devil is not the only obstacle we may face when dealing with faith. We must meditate on God's word and surround ourselves with like-minded believers. We cannot afford to keep company with doubting, negative-talking, unbelieving people.

We must also guard our minds. The devil will try to put unpleasant thoughts into our heads. The devil will try to convince us that God is not going to do what He promised. The devil may place a thought into someone's mind, "It's been five years and you are still not married."

The Bible states:

"We must cast down imaginations and every thought that exalts itself against the knowledge of God and bringing every thought into captivity to the obedience of Christ."

II Corinthians 10:5

We all should realize that just because the devil puts a thought into our minds doesn't mean we have to ponder on it. Think on the things of God.

"Finally brethren, whatsoever things are true, whatsoever things are honest, whatsoever things are just, whatsoever things are pure, whatsoever things are of a good report: If there be any virtue and if there be any praise, think on these things."

Philippians 4:8

Faith also requires confession. Death and life are in the power of the tongue: they that love it shall eat the fruit thereof. One must say what God's word says. Jesus instructs us that we will have what we confess. Even when a person doesn't feel like they are healed, they must continue to speak God's word, "By His stripes we are healed." If our finances are lacking speak the word over that situation, "I have abundance and no lack." Confess that your children will serve the Lord. Confess that your spouse or loved one will come to know the Lord. Some may reason in their minds that this is lying. No, we are confessing God's promises. We must not deny the physical situation or circumstances, but simply stand on the promises of the Almighty God.

"Call those things that be not as though they were."
Romans 4:17

Decisions Require Responsibility

I said before that the single most powerful thing that God has given us is the power of choice. But one consequence we must understand is that our decisions make us responsible for our destiny. I have found that many people don't want to be responsible for their decisions. Many people won't make a decision because they don't want to be responsible for their decisions. However, to not decide *is* to decide. Every decision you make is your decision. The decision to not do anything, or not choose anything, or not decide anything is a decision in itself.

After Adam and Eve ate the fruit and God came looking for Adam, Adam said, "the woman you gave me..." He placed the blame on God. But *he* made the decision to eat the fruit.

People get advice from other people and, if the situation doesn't go well, they blame the person who gave them the advice. But it was their decision to follow the advice or not. You must understand that even if you take advice from someone, the ultimate decision is in your hands. I don't care who gives you the advice - your pastor, a friend, your mother, your father, prophet, teacher - it doesn't matter. It is time we grew up and took responsibility for our own actions.

I recently read a case where a man was awarded millions of dollars after suing a cigarette company because he got cancer. He had smoked all his life and said it was the cigarette company's fault that he had cancer. How crazy; the cigarette company didn't force him to smoke. He did not want to take responsibility for his actions.

I have also seen cases where someone told someone else, "The Lord told me so-and-so is going to be your husband." This is very dangerous. I am sure that if the Lord can tell them, He can tell you too. The first thing that goes wrong in the marriage, and they will be blaming the person who told them, "The Lord said..." Regardless of anyone's advice, it was still your decision. I am trying to get you to see that you alone are responsible for your decisions.

People try to place the blame on their parents, their environment, their race, their government, their society, or even on God. Adam blamed God, Eve blamed the serpent, and the serpent turned and there was no one else to blame. When you make a decision, you must say, "This is my choice, and I will take responsibility for my actions." God will guide us and direct us, but He wants us to be responsible for our decisions and not play the blame game.

Decisions Are Determined By Priorities

You can tell a person's priorities by the decisions they make. If a person says, "God is a priority in my life," yet they don't study the Word of God, or the only time they pray is at meals, and instead of being in church they are out on their boat, you can plainly see God is not a priority in their life. The decisions you make will determine your priorities. I've seen people who said their family was a priority in life, but when they have the time to spend with them they were doing something else. I've heard people say their health is a priority, yet they never exercise, and at every opportunity they are at Burger King, or McDonald's. They always have an excuse for why they didn't make it to the gym. People have said getting out of debt was a priority, but they refused to get on a budget, or they couldn't resist the sale at the mall. If you say something is a priority in your life, look at the decisions you are making concerning that area, and you can determine by your decisions if it really is a priority.

Timely Decisions

"And they rose early in the morning and went up to the top of the mountain, saying "Here we are, and we will go up to the place which the Lord has promised, for we have sinned!" And Moses said, "Now why do you transgress the command of the Lord? For this will not succeed. Do not go up, lest you will be defeated by your enemies, For the Lord is not among you. For the Am-a-lek-ites and the Canaan-ites are there before you, and you shall fall by the sword; because you have turned away from the Lord, the Lord will not be with you." But they presumed to go up to

the mountaintop. **Nevertheless, neither the Ark of the Covenant of the Lord nor Moses departed from the camp. Then the Am-a-lek-ites and the Canaan-ites who dwelt in that mountain came down and attacked them, and drove them back as far as Hormah."**

Numbers 14:40-45

God had promised the children of Israel the land that flows with milk and honey. He instructed them to take the land. The twelve spies came back after surveying the land, and all but two had a negative report. Ten of the spies said the land was inhabited with giants, and they could not take it. Joshua and Caleb said, "We are well able to take the land!" The ten spies were going by what they *saw*. Joshua and Caleb were going by what God said.

We must stand on what the Word of God says, and not what we see. When the children of Israel did not take the land when God told them to, God then informed Moses of the judgment that was going to come upon them. After they found out about the judgment, they decided to go and take the land; but it was too late. Moses told them not to go because the Lord was not with them. They went anyway and the Am-a-lek-ites and the Canaan-ites smote them down.

We must be able to listen and discern the Lord's voice above all else. All too often we think that the Lord will open a door and then leave it open until we decide to walk through it. There are certain opportunities that God will present to us that we must act upon at that particular instant, or risk the chance of losing those opportunities forever. Some of us choose not to think negatively like this, but it is reality. We prefer to think that God will be merciful because He loves us, and that He has to give us one more chance. Yes, God is all of these things, merciful, slow to anger and more. However, there may be limitations when it concerns our willingness to act. We sometimes take God's mercy for granted. Time and time again the children of Israel had seen God come through for them. Yet, all they did was murmur, complain, and doubt God. May I remind you that God is not on our time schedule, we are on His. We want God to do things when we want them done. It doesn't work that way. We need to be ready to move when God says move. God knows more than we know. This may be a revelation to some people. I hate to think about some of the opportunities that people have lost out on because they didn't move when God instructed them to. I read a book by Joyce Meyer, and she recounted how she remembered when the Lord told her to go on television, and she said it was not a good time. The Lord replied that if she didn't take the opportunity now, this opportunity would not be given to her again. Dr. John Maxwell made a statement that timing is as important as making the right choice. He said, "The wrong decision at the wrong time = disaster. The wrong decision at the right time = mistake. The right decision at the wrong time = un-acceptance. The right decision at the right time = success." God is not interested in when we think the time is right, but whether or not we are willing to listen when He says the time is right. Our timing is never the right timing. We like to make decisions when we *feel* everything is perfect. We say we will get more involved in church when the children are grown. We will go back to school when our finances are in order. We will buy a house when we have the right job. We will have kids when we can afford them. We make decisions based on what we see. The Bible says, "We walk by faith, not by sight."

I remember hearing a story of a man who was called to full time ministry. The Lord told him to sell his house and go to seminary. The man didn't see how this could work. He had a wife and three kids and a good job. It didn't make sense to quit his job, sell his home and move his family. But he listened to God, and did what others might have thought not to be very sensible. He became a successful pastor and did what God instructed him to do. He had to decide to follow God's instruction, even though it didn't seem logical at the time. We must be close enough to God so that when He tells us to move, we move. So many people ask, "How can I tell if it is God's voice I hear?" Jesus said, "My sheep hear my voice." Many people don't know the voice of God because they don't spend time with Him. If I talk to you on the telephone on a regular basis, I learn to know your voice when I hear it. However, if I don't talk to you often, I might ask who is calling when you call. Many Christians don't talk to God on a regular basis, so they don't recognize His voice.

So often you hear people say that they are praying about certain situations. They might reason within themselves that they've been praying for this certain thing for the last five years without an answer. Don't misunderstand me; it is very important to pray about most circumstances. However, there are some things that we don't have to pray about. We don't have to pray about going to the bathroom, nor do we have to pray about eating. These things come naturally. I am not saying we should choose a marriage partner overnight, or move to another state without prayer. I am rather stating that some people use prayer as a cop out. Most of us know in our spirits when the Lord is prompting us to do something. Our inward witness is a sure guide. However, some people use the excuse that they are praying about their actions to avoid making decisions. We hear what God is instructing us to do, but we are not ready to follow Him. It may not necessarily be because we don't want to listen to God's instruction, but rather we allow fear to be an obstacle. One of the biggest reasons why many people don't act on the word of God spoken to their lives is fear.

" For God hath not given us a spirit of fear; but of power, and of love, and of a sound mind."

II Timothy 1:7

We must stand on the word of God and overcome fear. I heard a saying once, "Feel the fear and do it anyway." If God is directing us we have no need to fear. Stand on the word of God. Be sensitive to the leading of the Spirit. Spend time with God, and move when God says move.

So many times we have made decisions too quickly or too slowly. How many times have we reproached ourselves if only we had waited, or asked ourselves if we should have started sooner? There have been people who put off accepting Christ and now may be in hell. We must listen to God and make timely decisions.

Purpose in Your Heart

"But Daniel purposed in his heart that he would not defile himself with the portion of the king's meat, nor with the wine which he drank; therefore he requested of the prince of the eunuchs that he might not defile himself."

Daniel 1:8

The Bible says that Daniel purposed in his heart. When the Bible uses the word heart, it's talking about your spirit. It's not talking about your physical heart. I have come to the conclusion that real decisions are decisions made from the heart. You have heard the saying, "Let's get to the heart of the matter," or in other words, the things that are of real importance. Daniel purposed in his heart, not his head. When you get something in your heart, it's hard to remove it. That's why it's important that we are led by our spirit, not our emotions. Decisions made by the emotions normally don't last. How many times have we said we were going to lose weight, we start to diet and exercise, and we may lose weight, but a month or two later we have gained the weight back. We see a person on fire for the things of God, and one month later they are no longer in church. We see people make a commitment, and when storms come they fall by the wayside. Why? Because they have not purposed in their heart that no matter what happens, they're going to hang in there. When you make a decision, you must set up walls to protect those decisions. For example, if you decide you are not going to drink anymore, you must set up walls of protection. Don't go to places where they are serving alcohol. Don't hang around people who are drinking. You must make choices that are going to protect your decisions. I remember one time I was trying to lose weight, I would buy cookies and pop, and say that it was for when company came over. You know what happened? Company never seemed to see those cookies or pop. When I look at Daniel and the three Hebrew boys, I see people who made decisions and stuck with them. We must remember these boys were between the ages of 15 and 17. I am sure they had talked to each other before they were enslaved, and said, "No matter what happens, we will not bow down to false gods, even if it means death." Two people can get saved; one grows in the things of God, and one walks away from the things of God. One purposed in his heart, the other one didn't. Purpose in your heart, set up walls of protection, and make a quality decision. I must set up walls to protect the decisions that I made. There are certain places I cannot go, certain people I cannot surround myself with, certain music I must not listen to. When we make decisions and then do not follow through with our actions, we must ask ourselves the question, "Have I purposed this in my heart?" We must first purpose in our hearts above all that we have a desire to do God's will, and then we must take action and carry out the *will of God.*

Chapter 5

Spirit-Led Decisions

"For as many as are led by the Spirit of God, they are the sons of God."

Romans 8:14

We are a threefold being. We are spirits that have a soul and live in a body. Your spirit man is the real you. Your soul is your mind, your will and your emotions. Your body simply houses your spirit and soul. As a born again Christian, God talks to us through our spirit. God will not speak to your emotions or your body. The man or woman who hasn't accepted Jesus as their Lord and Savior can't hear from God because they are spiritually dead.

"But the natural man receiveth not the things of the spirit of God: for they are foolishness unto him: neither can he know them, because they are spiritually discerned."

I Corinthians 2:14

Before you become born again, your emotions and your flesh lead you. Whatever flesh wants, flesh gets. Flesh wants ice cream, therefore flesh gets ice cream. Flesh wants a new car, so flesh gets it. Flesh wants sex, flesh gets it, and it can be fornication or adultery. But when we are born again, our spirit comes into play in the decision-making process. Your spirit man is now alive, whereas before it was dead. The Bible says:

"If any man be in Christ he is a new creature, old things are passed away and behold all things are become new."
II Corinthians 5:17

So now your flesh or soul realm should no longer lead you. However, despite their new birth many Christians continue to be led by their body and soul instead of their spirit. We act on our five senses of touch, taste, smell, seeing and hearing all too often. We tend to be more body and soul conscious than we are spirit conscious. Now that we are born again, our spirit and flesh are at war. If the flesh says, "I want to slap Brother Jones", your spirit should say, "That is not walking in love, and that is not of God." The flesh answers back and says; "He shouldn't have said what he said." The spirit says, "You must walk in love and forgiveness." So, what do you do then? Well your soul will become the deciding factor. The decision your soul makes will depend on you. Remember I said your soul is your mind, your will, and your emotions. In Romans 12:2, the Bible tells us not to be conformed to this world, but to be transformed by the renewing of our minds. How much you have renewed your mind will determine what your soul decides. If you have filled your mind with the Word of God and the things of God, your soul will lean toward your spirit side. But if you have not renewed your mind, and you are still thinking like the world, your soul will side with your flesh. So it is very important that you renew your mind with the Word. Remember, Proverbs 23:7 says that as a man thinketh in his heart, so is he. Think on the things of God.

The primary way that God leads us is through the inward witness. This is the number one way we are led. What is your inward witness? Your inward witness is the voice of your spirit. I'll give you an example. A friend of mine, who is a born-again Christian, got off work late one night, about 1:00 or 2:00 o'clock in the morning. He said something on the inside of him told him to take a different exit home. He reasoned in himself and took the way he normally goes home. He didn't take the exit he felt prompted to take and within five minutes he had fallen asleep and a truck hit him and tore his car to pieces. He was banged up a little, nothing serious. Had he listened to his inward witness this may never have happened. I know of people who were getting married, and something on the inside told them not to go through with it. But they did, and ended up in terrible situations. I'll give you another example: there was a man who had invested a lot of money in a particular stock. Something on the inside told him to go and cash in everything. He began to reason in himself that everything was going great, his stocks were up. There was no reason to be alarmed. But his inward witness continued to unction him to cash in his stocks. He followed the leading of his inward witness and two days later the market crashed. I heard of a situation of a man who was getting ready for a trip home on an airplane. He said he received an unction on the inside of him, telling him not to get on the airplane. He didn't take the flight, and the plane crashed. His inward witness told him not to get on the plane.

I can think of many times that my spirit prompted me to do something, or not to do something. The times I obeyed, I prospered; the times I disobeyed, I paid a price for it. Some people ignore the guidance of their inner witness, despite what they hear or are prompted to do. Some hear and obey the voice of their spirit. Some disobey, although they hear, and some don't hear. Why do you think some people hear the voice of their spirit?

Well, the spirit has to be developed. Just like the natural body can be developed through exercise, likewise, your spirit can be developed. When we become born again, I believe the number one thing we must do is renew our minds. Romans 12:2, says, "be not conformed to this world but be transformed by the renewing of your mind." When you get saved, your mind needs to be renewed with the Word of God. Before we get saved, we are more familiar with following the things of the world. I got saved when I was twenty-seven years old. That means I have had twenty-seven years of the world's system of thought pumped into me. I've been saved for seven years now. I can't block out twenty-seven years of thinking and training in the ways of the world in one night. We must make up our minds that we will do whatever it takes to renew our minds. I must feed myself on the Word of God, pray, and fellowship with God and like-minded Christians on a daily basis. I must make the decision to create an environment that will allow me to build up my spirit. I must watch the types of music I listen to, and television programs I that watch. I can no longer go to some of the places I used to go, or hang out with the people I used to hang out with. Proverbs 23:7 says for as he thinketh in his heart, so is he. What you think on you will become. Every action starts with a thought. Paul told us what to think on in Philippians 4:8:

"Finally, brethren, whatsoever things are true, whatsoever things are honest, whatsoever things are just, whatsoever things are pure, whatsoever things are lovely, whatsoever things are of a good report: if there be any virtue, and if there be any praise, think on these things."

Philippians 4:8

You must spend time with God so you can learn His ways. When you learn His ways, it is not hard to figure out what is not His way. Another way to develop your spirit is to pray in other tongues. For if I pray in an unknown tongue, MY SPIRIT prayeth, but my understanding is unfruitful. Your spirit is built up when you pray in other tongues. You must also keep your spirit clear, and not cluttered. A car can't get in the garage if it is full of stuff. God can't communicate well with your spirit if it is cluttered. Keep a clean spirit to allow God clear communication with you. We must take care of the matters of the heart, so our hearts won't be full when God wants to talk to us. I believe this is the most important way we should make decisions. I haven't even begun to touch this subject, however, if you would like more information concerning this matter, Brother Kenneth E. Hagin has books and tapes on this subject matter. There are also other good ministers of the gospel who have taught on this matter. In conclusion, when making decisions, be led by the Spirit.

Decisions of Convenience

Convenience is one of the biggest reasons people make bad decisions. The word convenience means to make things easier. There's a convenience store around the corner from my home. It is easier to go to that store, but it will cost me more. The prices are higher but I might not have to wait as long or drive as far. I know of a situation where a friend of mine goes to a church that is about ten minutes from her house. The problem is that she is not getting fed the Word. She doesn't feel as if she is growing as a Christian. She has told me that she doesn't feel close to her pastor, even though it is a small church. However, she knows of a church that she has visited, and really enjoyed. She watches this church on television and listens to them on the radio. She has been fed tremendously from this church. But the church is an hour's drive from her house. She is not willing to drive the hour to get fed the Word of God because it is not convenient. I would say her spiritual well-being should be more important than a ten-minute drive.

I know people who have gotten married because of convenience. One person may have a lot of money, a good job, or a nice house. I once heard a young lady say about her husband; "I am not really happy or in love with him, but he pays the bills." There are a lot of people who live in what I call a comfort zone. They will never reach their full potential. If Abraham had not left his comfort zone, he would not have reached his full potential for God. Elisha left great wealth, family, and friends to follow Elijah. To get what God had for him, he had to come out of his comfort zone.

Don't get me wrong, convenience can be good. For example, I like microwave ovens, I like cruise control, and I like air conditioning. Currently I drive an hour each way to the church I attend. However, I have made plans to move to that town because it will be more convenient to me. I am trying to point out in this chapter that people make bad decisions because of convenience. You must put forth great effort to fulfill the destiny that God has ordained for your life. Remember the definition I gave you earlier for convenience is to make things easier. I want to challenge you to come out of your comfort zone. In order to get what God has for you it is going to cost you something. If you are going to tap into greatness, you can't make decisions based on convenient situations. Rise up and be all that God has called you to be.

Chapter 6

God is No Respecter of Persons

<u>Then Peter opened his mouth and said:</u>

"Of a truth I perceive that God is no respecter of persons."

Acts 10:34

Some people are mistaken in their perception that God has favorites. In school we have what people call "a teacher's pet." This means that the teacher has a favorite student, and that student may receive special treatment. When it comes to God, there are no teacher's pets. <u>The Bible tells us:</u>

"For God so loved the world that He gave His only begotten son that <u>whosoever</u> believeth in Him should not perish but have everlasting life."

John 3:16

The word I want you to concentrate on is **whosoever**, which means *who-so-ever* will. God is a God of covenants, and whoever enters into covenant with Him will receive His blessings.

Jesus died for every single person on earth, not just a select few. It is not a matter of who you rub elbows with. We all have a choice to make. There are too many members of the Body of Christ making excuses today for their shortcomings.

My Bible states:

"I can do all things through Christ which strengths me."

Philippians 4:13

I love this characteristic about God. He lets us know that it is up to us if we are to succeed or fail. It's our choice! I hear so many people say that they wish they were like so-and-so; or they wish they had the anointing like such-and-such. They feel that he or she is so blessed, but they don't see themselves as blessed. I like what Bishop T.D. Jakes said, "If you want what I have, you must do what I do." People want things that they are not willing to work for in order to get them. Often when people find out what the other person has had to go through to get what they have, they become discouraged. Many times they change their minds because they are not willing to work as hard to get what these other people have. They are not willing to work as hard to achieve their own success.

There is always a price to pay in order to get what you want in life. Pastor Robyn Gool, Pastor of Victory Christian Center, Charlotte, NC, once said that when he first got started in his ministry, he asked God if he could have a ministry like Fred Price, Oral Roberts, Kenneth Copeland and Kenneth Hagin. The Lord answered him with this thought: "Only if you are willing to do what they did!" Today he has a very special ministry that is reaching Charlotte, NC, and other parts of the world as well. I guess he was willing to pay the price. This is a question that we need to ask ourselves. Are we willing to do what it takes to be successful?

God has laws and principles, and whosoever abides by these shall receive the rewards. Whoever will be obedient to the Word of God will receive His blessings. God doesn't state that He will bless me because I am a good guy. Rather, He blesses me when I obey His Word. I must be obedient. I must also work hard to fulfill the purpose God has ordained for my life. God is not holding out on you. God is simply showing you that if you do not put forth the effort, you won't fulfill your destiny, nor attain the success you desire. An example of this would be if you were to ask your boss for a raise at work, and he informed you that certain objectives needed to be met in order for you to get your raise. You would not expect your boss to give you the raise until the objectives were achieved. In the same fashion some parents tell their children they will be rewarded if they obey the rules of the home. At times the children do not comply, yet they are rewarded anyway. God doesn't reward in this manner. God rewards obedience. Don't get me wrong, God is a God of grace and mercy, and He blesses at times even when we don't deserve it. But understand this is not the norm. The Word of God states that,

"He is a rewarder of them that diligently seek Him."
Hebrews 11:6

God is a rewarder. God is a giver. God is a God of love; however, don't mistake God's love for God's blessings. God's love is unconditional. But His Word outlines certain principles that govern His blessings. The Word of God states that if you bring your tithes and offerings to the storehouse, He will open up the windows of heaven and pour you out blessings. If you do not tithe, nor give offerings to God, you should not expect your finances to prosper. God still loves you, but your blessings may be limited because His Word states that we should bring our tithes and offerings to God. If you want eternal life, you must accept Jesus as your Lord and Savior. God loves us regardless, but we must accept Jesus, or spend eternity in hell. You hear people speak sometimes about a loving God that wouldn't send anyone to hell. He certainly would not. However, we send ourselves to hell if we reject Jesus. It does not matter if you feed the poor, clothe the naked, never steal, never kill, nor lie. We can still die and go to hell if we deny Jesus as our Lord and Savior. God instructs us that we must be born again.

We hear people say it is not God's will for everyone to be healed. Or, it's not God's will for everyone to be prosperous. This is not what my Bible tells me. My Bible reads:

"Beloved, I wish above all things that you may prosper and be in health, even as your soul prospers."
John 3:2

As our soul prospers, we are prospered, in health, and in wealth. As we grow in spirit, we grow in other aspects of our lives. We grow in spirit by continuing in the Word. We must continue in the Word.

Jesus also said:

"If you continue in my word, then you are my disciples indeed; and, you shall know the truth and the truth shall make you free."
John 8:31

The word *if* implies that there is a condition that has to be met. So many people quote the latter part of this scripture. However, in order to know the truth, and be set free, you must continue in the Word.

My favorite scripture is Joshua 1:8:

"This book of the law shall not depart out of thy mouth; but thou shalt meditate therein both day and night, that thou mayest observe to do according to all that is written therein: for then thou shalt make thy way prosperous and then thou shalt have good success."

Joshua 1:8

God instructs us that in order to be prosperous and to be successful, we must meditate on the Word both day and night, and do what is written in it. We cannot let the Book of the Law depart from our mouth. In other words, there are conditions that we must meet in order to gain success. I personally choose to meet these conditions. How about you, what choice are you making?

"But by the grace of God I am what I am: and His grace which was bestowed upon me was not in vain; But I laboured more abundantly than they all: yet not I but the grace of God which was with me."

I Corinthians 15:10

Paul is saying that he is what he is by the grace of God. Paul is also saying that he laboured more abundantly than the other apostles did. He is saying that he worked harder, he studied more, and he visited more places and preached the gospel more than the others did. He is saying that yes, the grace of God was upon him, but he has also paid a price. We know that Paul was one of the greatest preachers of the gospel, ever. I have even heard people jokingly say that Paul was the 4th member of the Godhead. Paul wrote more than two thirds of the New Testament. Paul did a lot, but Paul also suffered a lot. We see some of the things Paul suffered in 2 Corinthians 11:23-28. Paul paid a great price to fulfill the purpose that God had for his life. We see in 2 Timothy 4:7 that Paul finished his course. He was willing to pay the price.

51

God is no respecter of persons. If you are willing to pay the price you too, like the Apostle Paul, can say, "I have finished my course."

One thing I would like to make clear is that although God is not a respecter of persons, and we say that God will do for you what He has done for another, this doesn't mean you will get the exact same things, or ministry gifts and talents, as someone else. This doesn't mean that if one person is preaching to thousands then you will preach to thousands. That may not be God's plan and purpose for your life. What this means is that God has provided us with every spiritual blessing in heavenly places, however, it is up to us to receive them *by our obedience* in order for them to become a reality in our lives. God has given you special gifts and talents and abilities. It is up to you to fulfill your destiny. God may not deal with all his children just the same but He does deal fairly.

Love is a Decision

"For God so loved the world that He gave His only begotten son that whosoever believeth on Him should not perish but have everlasting life."

John 3:16

Most people think that love is a feeling. This is not correct. Love is a decision. Think about how often you actually feel like loving people. If love were simply a feeling, then there would not be a great deal of love going around. The Bible tells us that God so loved the world that He gave His only Son. Do you think that God felt like loving us considering the way we behaved? No, God made a *decision* to love us. When your children behave in a manner that displeases or embarrasses you, you don't always *feel* like loving them. However, you continue to love them despite their actions, because you made a decision to love them regardless of how you felt at the time. A spouse may not feel like loving their husband or wife all the time. But love is not a feeling; it is a decision. Do you think Jesus *felt* like leaving Heaven, only to come to earth and endure the suffering He had to bear? No, Jesus made a decision to come to earth and be our Savior, and He loved us unconditionally. I don't know about you, but I have run across many people who were not very lovable.

There are three types of love. The first is phileo, meaning friendship. Phileo is the type of love people share because they have certain characteristics and beliefs in common. People who get along together real well, and have a lot of similarities, share this kind of love (I love you because you love me). The second type of love is eros, deriving from the English word erotic. This is simply a lustful love. A person may lust after another because they feel they can fulfill their sexual desires. Love displayed in this way is only temporal, because the person is desired only as an object. And once the other person's desire is fulfilled, they don't want to have any more involvement with that person. The third type of love is agape, expressing the God kind of love. This kind of love is unconditional (I love you regardless). As Christians we are to always seek and express agape love.

God gave us a free will. We have the right to choose. God gave Adam and Eve a choice. He gives you and me a choice. The choice can include a person's decision to reject Him. God will not force us to love Him. God desired that Adam and Eve express their love by obeying Him. God feels the same way about you and me. People base love on how they feel, and by what others can do for them. We should not want someone to love us because of what we can do for him or her, or what he or she can do for us. We should want them to love us even if we never do anything for them. Of course, we know that doing things for someone comes along with the territory. As Christians we are to love everyone unconditionally, as Jesus loved us. If a person spit in my face, I must still love them, not because I feel like it, but rather because I made a decision to love them despite their actions. I once heard Fred Price state that you must love some people by faith. Believe me it takes a lot of faith to love some of the people I have met. So remember love is not a feeling, but rather a decision.

Choosing a Mate is Your Decision

Most people think that there is only one special person in the whole entire world for them to marry. This is not true. If this were true, God would be choosing for us, and that would be going against our will. As we talked in previous chapters, God gives us the ability and the right to make our own decisions, and that includes choosing a mate. A lot of people go around saying, "I claim this person, or that person, as my husband or wife." Or, "The Lord told me so-and-so was going to be my spouse." This is not scriptural. If this were the case, then God would be going against a person's right to say no. Many people mistakenly believe that a word of prophecy was spoken to them concerning a certain person that God has chosen to be their spouse. Later that person discovers that the person is already married with three children. I believe that God has prepared many different people that you can discover as your perfect mate. If you stay on the right road, eventually you will come across the right person for you. It will still be your choice as to whether or not you choose them as a mate.

Oftentimes, what happens is people get off the road looking for Mr. or Mrs. Right, as opposed to staying on the road and running into that right person. Regardless of whom you marry, you still need to work hard at making your marriage successful. Most people think that if they could just find the right person, then everything would be peaches and cream from that moment on. People conclude that God _sent_ them their mate. When the marriage fails, and ends in separation or divorce, they begin to question God as to why He _sent_ them the person in the first place. God didn't choose them, you did! Like I stated before, God will guide you and direct you, but He will never choose for you! So many people are looking for a mate to fulfill them. No, a person can never fulfill you; only God can. Your mate should complement you. Adam was in the garden doing what God had called him to do. He didn't look around and say, "I need someone to fulfill me." God decided he needed a *helpmeet.* Eve complemented Adam; she did not complete him. So many people don't think that they are complete unless they find a mate. You should be complete first, before you seek a mate. God's mathematics, and His equations are not like ours. God determines that 1+1=1. One *whole* man plus one *whole* woman equals one *whole* relationship. If you have half a man and half a woman, you only have one half a relationship. $1/2 + 1/2 = 2/4$, which in its lowest denomination is only equal to $1/2$. We must be complete in God before we decide to get married. It is up to you then to choose the right mate.

Predestined

Some years ago there was a teaching that was going around about predestination. The teaching stated that God had predetermined that some people were destined to go to heaven, and some people were destined to go to hell.

What this tells me is that there are a lot of people who have not read the Bible:

For God *so loved* the world that he gave his only begotten Son, that whosoever believeth in him should not perish but have eternal life.

John 3:16

Look at what probably the most well-known scripture to man tells us. It says that God so loved the world that He gave His only begotten Son, that whosoever believeth... STOP right there. What does whosoever mean? It means *who ever decides to believe in Jesus* will have everlasting life. Well, if you were predestined to go to heaven or hell, you wouldn't have a choice. I said in chapter one that the single most powerful thing that we as people possess is the power of choice. I believe that God is a good God. And if that is the case, then why would He want a bad outcome for me or anybody else?

For I know the thoughts that I think towards you, saith the Lord, thoughts of peace, and not of evil, to give you an expected end.

Jeremiah 29:11

God has a plan and a purpose that He desires to see fulfilled. He has included you and I in the plan, if we are willing to participate. God created your end before your beginning. Your life doesn't begin and then God says, "Go here, do this, don't do that." No, your life was planned before the foundation of the world!

According as he hath chosen us in him before the foundation of the world, that we should be holy and without blame before him in love. Having predestinated us, unto the adoption of children by Jesus Christ to himself, according to the good pleasure of his will.

Ephesians 4:1, 5

He chose you before the foundation of the world. So, yes, you were predestined. You were predestined to do God's will. I don't see any instance where the will of God for your life is bad. Look at what Ephesians 2:10 says:

For we are his workmanship, created in Jesus Christ unto good works, which God hath before ordained that we should walk in then.

Ephesians 2:10

Look at what God told Jeremiah:

Then the word of the Lord came unto me, saying, before I formed thee in the belly I knew thee; and before thou cometh forth out of the womb I sanctified thee, and I ordained thee a prophet unto the nations.

Jeremiah 1:4, 5

God tells Jeremiah, "Before you were born, I had a predetermined destiny for your life." It's funny though, because I never see anyone with a bad predetermined destiny. Now you hear people say, "If God had this wonderful plan for such-and-such's life, why did they die like that?" The fact of the matter is we still have choices to make. You also hear when a person dies, it was just their time. Well was it? You mean to tell me that the 16 year old who was stabbed to death, after being brutally beaten, that was God's way for him to die? Or that person that overdosed on drugs, was it their time - forget the fact that they were only 20 years old? What about when the Bible says that God promises long life? There are things that happen in life as a result of the choices we make. God has a plan mapped out for your life. It's the best plan that you could ever imagine. But if you are going to see that plan fulfilled, you must make the right choices.

Chapter 7

Do not Compare Yourself

For we dare not make ourselves of the number, or compare ourselves with some that commend themselves, but they measuring themselves by themselves, and comparing themselves among themselves, are not wise.

II Corinthians 10:12

One reason people never fulfill their destiny and complete the course that God has mapped out for their lives, is that they do not appreciate who they are. What am I saying? I am saying people hold themselves back by comparing themselves to other people. The Apostle Paul says this is not wise. I told you before that you are unique. No one else has your fingerprints. You are an original. When God created you, He broke the mold. When I hear people say they wish they were so and so, I think how sad. That is a slap in God's face. I would not want to be anybody but Ralph Douglas Phifer. I love being me. If people would spend as much time developing their gifts, talents, abilities, and finding out what God has created them to do, there would be no time for comparing themselves to someone else. God is not a respecter of persons. We look at people like Billy Graham and say,

"Wow, I wish I could be like Dr. Graham." Well God has an assignment for you that is just as important as Dr. Graham. Two things God is very interested in: faithfulness and obedience. If God told you to go to the ghetto, lead ten drug dealers to Christ, and you do it, guess what? You will receive that same reward as Dr. Graham. You may not preach to thousands or have your own T.V. ministry. But if you do what God called you to do, you will be rewarded accordingly. You are just as important to God.

For as the body is one, and hath many members, and all the members of that one body, being many are one body; so also is Christ

I Corinthians 12:12

The Scripture is saying that there is one body that has many members. We are the body of Christ. Christ is the head. Can your body walk around without your head? What is more important: your ears or eyes, hands or feet, taste or smell? There was a pastor who was upset because Fred Price has about 20,000 members. He said, he wished he could have a congregation that size. He was asked how many members he had. He said 600. He was also asked what the size of the town he lived in was; He said 900. He had 600 members in a town of 900. Fred Price is in Los Angeles, California, where there are millions of people. You add up the percentage. But do you see what I am trying to say? Let me tell you another story. There was an evangelist who held a crusade. At the end of the crusade, only one young boy came forth and gave his life to Christ. The evangelist considered that crusade a failure. That young boy was Billy Graham. I hardly consider that crusade a failure. We all play a big part in the big picture. Different people have different gifts and skills. It's up to us to find, develop, and use those gifts to be a blessing as well as fulfilling your purpose. Remember God created you for an assignment. No one can complete that assignment but you because that was what you were created to do. Focus on that assignment and do not compare yourself to others. Sometimes when we start comparing ourselves to others, we open the door to envy and jealousy. Most of the time if we knew what people went through to get to where they are, we would say no thank you. Find out what God has called you to do and dominate that area. If you are called to teach Sunday school, to drive the church bus, to work with the children's ministry, the ministry of helps, to start your own business, to clean bathrooms, or to pastor 20,000 people, be the best at what you do. Many people are not fulfilling their purpose in life because they feel like they do not matter. They feel they are insignificant. God is thinking about you.

For we are his workmanship created in Christ Jesus unto good works, which God hath before ordained that we should walk in them.

Ephesians 2:10

This is one of my favorite scriptures. I want you to think about it. You are God's workmanship. You were created by almighty God. I worked security at a museum. We had paintings by Rembrandt and sculptures by famous people. People would come up to me and say where are the paintings by Rembrandt or the paintings by so and so or the sculptures by such and such. They were so excited about seeing the work of some famous artist. I began to think about this scripture. I am God's workmanship. I am unique. Think about it. No one else in the world has your fingerprints. The people were so excited about what a man or woman had done. What about what God has done?

I will praise thee; for I am fearfully and wonderfully made; marvelous are thy works and that my soul knoweth right well

Psalm 139:14

60

You are fearfully and wonderfully made. God just did not throw you together. He took his time with you. He was very careful. Each little detail put in place. I do not care what people have said about you. I do not care what they told you. They may have said you would never amount to anything. They may have said they wished you were never born. They may said have that the world would be a better place without you. But it doesn't matter what they say. What only matters is what God says. It's not what people think about you, but what God thinks about you. If I take a $10,000 diamond ring, say you are worthless, you should have never been made, and throw it in the garbage, guess what? It is still worth $10,000. So what people say or think about you doesn't change your value.

For I know the thoughts that I think towards you, saith the Lord, thoughts of peace, and not of evil, to give you an expected end.

Jeremiah 29:11

God has a plan and purpose for your life. You are important to him. He's thinking about you, the purpose, and plan He has ordained for your life. You can make a difference. Submit your life to God and He will show you your destiny.

Chapter 8

You have an assignment

And, behold, I come quickly; and my reward is with me, to give every man according as his work shall be.

Revelations 22:12

You are responsible for your life. You have a purpose and it is up to you to find that purpose. While you are here on this earth you have an assignment. Jesus was here on assignment. He said I am here to do the will of Him who sent me. God has equipped you with everything you need to complete your assignment. It's up to you: find, develop, reproduce, and distribute those gifts. In Matthew 25:14, 30, we see the parable of the talents. One servant was given five talents, another servant two talents, and another one talent. The servant with five talents traded and made five more talents. The servant with two traded also and earned two more talents. But the servant with one talent did nothing with his talent, and when the Lord returned, He rewarded them according to what they had done with their talents. Many people live life and never find their purpose for being here. They die with all their gifts, ideas, books, businesses, poems, sermons, and inventions still on the inside of them. The world never saw what God deposited on the inside of them.

I have fought a good fight. I have finished my course. I have kept the faith.

II Timothy 4:7

The Apostle Paul is coming to the end of his life; and he is saying that he has completed his assignment. What an awesome statement to make. How many people can come to the end of their life and say they did what they were put on this earth to do? Most people come to the end of their life and say, "I wish I could live my life over again." My friend, you do not have to be one of those people. Regardless of where you are in life right now, you can make a change. I do not care how old you are. God called Moses when he was 80 years old. Caleb was 85 when he said, "give me my mountain." If you have breath in your body, God can use you. It's not too late. I remember Kenneth Copeland saying that he told God, he felt bad because he did not get saved until he was 30. He said he wished he had been like brother Hagin who was saved and preaching at age 17. He said, "Where would my ministry be if I had not wasted all those years?" The Lord spoke to him and said right where it is now. In other words, the Lord said in Joel 2:25, "I will restore to you the years that the locust has eaten." And God can also restore to you the years that you have lost. You have an assignment.

Then the word of the Lord came unto me, saying before I formed thee in the belly I knew thee; and before thou camest forth out of the womb I sanctified thee, and I ordained thee a prophet unto the nations.

Jeremiah 1:45

God is telling Jeremiah before he was born, He had a plan for his life. He had an assignment for him to fulfill. He has an assignment for you also. The only one who can tell you what you were created for, is the One who created you. Give your life to God. Read and study His word. Pray on a daily basis. Seek a Bible believing and teaching church. Ask God, "Why am I here?" He will reveal to you your assignment.

A man's gift maketh room for him, and bringeth him before great men.

Proverbs 18:16

Your gifts are connected to your assignment. You do not decide what you want to be in life; you discover what you are. Everyone has an assignment to complete in his or her lifetime. God has equipped every one of us with gifts, talents, abilities, and skills that will help us to complete our assignment. It's up to us to find, develop, reproduce, and distribute those gifts. The problem is that, you have a lot of people wanting to do things that they are not equipped to do. One time, T.D. Jakes was asked how he was able to do so much traveling, holding conferences, guest speaking, writing books, and pastoring over 30,000 people. He said, "Because God has equipped me to do that." It seems too much for you because you are not equipped to do that. A lot of people are trying to do things they are not equipped to do. Do not keep your eyes on what other people are doing. Concentrate on your gifts and talents; and maximize them to the fullest. There are many people who are not walking in the call that God has ordained for their life. You have pastors that are supposed to be bus drivers. You have doctors that are supposed to be evangelists. You have prophets that are supposed to be Sunday school teachers. You have businessmen who are called to be pastors. We sometimes look at people and say, "Wow, I would do that." They see Benny Hinny and say, "I would like to have a healing ministry and be on television like that." Remember what I said earlier, you do not decide what you want to be; you discover who you are. I am not concerned with what God has called someone else to be. I just want to be what he has called me to be; and develop my gifts, talents, abilities, skills to the fullest, and use them to be a blessing to the world and to fulfill my destiny. How do you discover who you are?

Delight thyself also in the Lord and he shall give you the desire of thine heart.

Psalm 37:4

Most people have the wrong idea about God. They believe God wants them to do something that they do not have a desire to do. They say such things as, "If I get saved, God will call me to be a missionary to Africa." God would not call you to do something that you do not have a desire to do; when you do not have a desire to do something, you will not be very effective at doing it. When I first read Psalm 37:4, I thought it meant the Lord would give me the desires of my heart such as a six bedroom house and a Mercedes Benz, but that's not what that scripture is saying. It's saying, He will place a desire in your heart to do what he has called you to do. But in order for Him to do this, you must first delight in Him. That's the part of the scripture we do not pay much attention to. We must take pleasure in God. Spend time fellowshipping with Him, loving on Him, seeking His face, and becoming a part of His plan. The closer we get to Him, the more important His plan becomes a part of our life; and His desires become our desires. Another way to discover what your gifts is to get involved in your local church. People can sometimes see our gifts better than we can. I've had people tell me that I was gifted in an area I really did not pay much attention to, but because they could see me better than I saw myself, they recognized that gift that was operating in my life. I've seen people in offices that just did not seem to be what they were called to do. People can see the gifts in you, people like your pastor, other ministers of the gospel, church members, and friends. But if you do not get involved, it is hard to see what your gifts are. Joyce

Meyer said that she helped with children's ministry and she knew immediately that was not her gift. Find out what you enjoy doing. The things that we enjoy doing were given to us by God. You may enjoy visiting the elderly, serving people, or driving the church bus. On the other hand, look at what you do not like. It may make you mad to see children abused. So you may feel called to minister in that area. I have a friend who told me drugs destroyed her family, so she has a strong desire to reach out to drug addicts. The woman who started MADDs, Mothers Against Drunk Driving, child was killed by a drunk driver. She now puts her time in that area. What do you have a heart for? What stays on your mind most of the time? That's a good indication of where your gift may be. I know many people who went to Bible College thinking God had called them to be pastors and apostles, only to find out they were meant for the children's ministry and the ministry of helps, or vice versa. Continue to seek God's face and as the scripture says, your gift will make room for you. It will open doors, give you opportunities and bring you before great men.

Chapter 9

Prepare for the opportunity

And that servant, which knew his Lord's will, and prepared no himself, neither did according to his will, shall be beaten with many stripes.

Luke 12:47

One of the greatest things you can do when you find your purpose, is to prepare yourself for the opportunity that lies ahead. There is an old saying that states, "Preparation time is never wasted time." If you are going to be all God has called you to be, you must be prepared. When we look at the lives of men and women of God, we see they had times of preparation for what God was calling them to do. Moses was on the backside of the desert for 40 years, before he was ready to lead the children of Israel out of Egypt. Joshua was under Moses 39 years before he took over. David was anointed king at the age of 17, but did not take over the throne until he was 30. Elisha followed Elijah 10 years before he received a double portion. Paul the Apostle spent 17 years preparing for his calling. Look at our Lord Jesus. He spent 30 years preparing for a three and a half year ministry. So you see how important it is to prepare for your destiny. I am convinced that many marriages do not make it because of lack of preparation.

All the time is spent preparing for the wedding instead of the marriage. You will spend hundreds of dollars on a dress, but won't spend anything on some good books or tapes that teach you how to be a good wife or husband. We will spend thousands of dollars on limos, catering, flowers, but nothing on good material on how to live with a woman or a man. We spend nothing on the needs of a woman or the needs of a man and wonder why the divorce rate is so high. We have not prepared ourselves. If you want God to use you, you must prepare yourself. Ask yourself this question. If I was to receive an opportunity right now in my area of expertise, would I be ready? If you are called to preach and given an opportunity to preach, would you be ready? What about to sing? Could you do it? Or would you say, "can you let me do it next week?" If you said that, then how do you expect God to use you? In my principles on diligence, I said a diligent person is a person who prepares for an opportunity that does not exist. You should be prepared at all times. A fighter doesn't win a fight in the ring. He wins the fight before the fight, with his preparation. How you are prepared, will determine how you perform. If you plan to be victorious, then you must put forth the effort to prepare. What does a sports team do? They do not wait until the day of the game to get ready. They have spent time studying film of their opponents, going over their game plan, studying the weaknesses and strengths of the other team, getting themselves mentally and physically prepared. It's going to take time, effort, and sacrifice to prepare ourselves for the task that lies ahead. Michael Jordan said he practiced so hard, that when the game came, it was very easy. Remember what I said earlier, how you prepare will determine how you perform. What are you doing to develop your skills? How much time are you putting in studying and praying? It's better to be prepared for an opportunity that never happens, than to not be prepared and it does happen. It's like taking a test. If you have prepared and studied, you have that confidence. But if you have not studied, there's a bad feeling when you walk in to take the test. Let's prepare ourselves for what God has called us to do, so that we are not ashamed when we are called on to perform a certain task.

And shall Lay thee even with the ground, and thy children within thee; and they shall not leave in thee no stone upon another; because thou knewest not the time of thy visitation

Luke 19:44

The word opportunity means a fixed or definite period of time. It means season. We often see the word season in the Bible. It means a while or as we say a little while. The Bible says in Luke 4, that after the devil had finished tempting Jesus, he left him for a season, or should we say a specific amount of time. We have heard the phrase, the window of opportunity. We must climb through that window before it closes. There will be times in our lives that God will give us opportunities. And it's very important that we take advantage of these opportunities. What type of opportunities am I talking about? I am talking about showing the world and the devil that the child of God cannot be stopped. God has promised us many things. In order for us to walk in these promises, we must have opportunities. Think about some of the things that you are believing the Lord for. Think about some of the things you want to do for the Lord. Think about the call that God has on your life. In order for these things to come to pass, you have to have an opportunity. But not only do you have to have an opportunity, but you have to be prepared for the opportunity. Let's look at the situation concerning David and Goliath. David was a Shepard herding sheep. His father gave him some food to take his brothers, who were at war. Goliath had come out and challenged the army of

God. Everyone was afraid. The king had said whoever killed Goliath, his house would be free of taxes, he would get to marry the king's daughter, and great riches would be bestowed upon him. Not only that, but it would show everyone that God's people are superior because we serve the true and living God. I would say this is a big opportunity. David comes on the scene. He finds out what's going on and volunteers to fight the giant. The kings tells David he is no match for the giant. But David tells him, while he was tending the sheep a lion and bear attacked one of his lambs and he killed them. Notice what David said next. "The Lord that delivered the bear and the lion into my hands, will also deliver this uncircumcised Philistine into my hand also." Notice who his trust was in, not his own strength, but in the Lord's strength. I'll bet while David was out tending to the sheep, he was also spending time with the Lord; Praising and praying to God. He prepared himself for the opportunity, and when the opportunity arrived, he took full advantage of it. He killed Goliath, and the rest of the army fled when they saw their champion was dead. So many people want opportunities, but they are not prepared. Ask yourself, "Am I ready for the opportunity?" If you want a new position on your job, can you handle it? If you were called to preach, are you ready? You also must have the ability to recognize the opportunity. Many people are asking God for an opportunity, and they do not even recognize it when God gives it to them. You may be called to pastor, but God may tell you to usher for a while. You may say that's not what am I called to do. Before David defeated Goliath, he defeated the lion and bear. Why would God give you a thousand dollars if you do not tithe off of the hundred dollars? So not only do you need to be prepared for an opportunity when it comes, but you must be able to also recognize it when it comes. It may not come in the form you think. We have a tendency to think God will always give us another opportunity. That is not always the case.

Some opportunities come and are gone. God is merciful and a God of second, third, fourth, and sixth chances, but we can't always depend on those chances. So seize the opportunity now.

Stay Focused

The person who exercises his or her ability to stay focused, is the person that cannot be stopped. I want you to notice what I said. I said the person who exercises his or her ability to stay focused, is the person that cannot be stopped. I did not say the person who has the ability to stay focused, because we all have the ability to stay focused. Think about some point and time in your life, when you had a particular task that had to be done and you finished it. You may have had a test to study for; and you put everything else aside and focused on passing the test. And you passed it. You may have wanted to clean out the garage. I'll bet you can think of something you set your mind to completing and you did it. So you see we have the ability to stay focused, but we do not always exercise our ability to stay focused.

Jesus is our example in everything we do. And when we look at the life of Jesus, we see he had many opportunities to exercise his ability to stay focused and he did.

Now his parents went to Jerusalem every year at the feast of the Passover. And when he was twelve years old, they went up to Jerusalem after the custom of the feast. And when they had fulfilled the days, as they returned, the child Jesus tarried behind in Jerusalem; and Joseph and his mother knew not of it. But they, supposing him to have been in the company, went a day's journey; and they sought him among their kinsfolk and acquaintance. And when they found him not, they turned back again to Jerusalem, seeking

him. And it came to pass, that after three days they found him in the temple, sitting in the midst of the doctors, both hearing them, and asking them questions. And all that heard him were astonished at his understanding and answers. And when they saw him, they were amazed: and his mother said unto him, Son, why hast thou thus dealt with us? Behold, thy father and I have sought thee sorrowing. And he said unto them, how is it that ye sought me? Wist ye not that I must be about my Father's business?

Luke 2: 41-49

Here we see Jesus at the age of twelve focusing on the plan and purpose that God had ordained for his life. He's exercising his ability to stay focused. He knew what his purpose was at an early age and he went after it. At the age when other kids were out playing, Jesus was in the temple hearing God and asking Him questions. Ecclesiastes 12:1 says, "Remember now thou Creator in the days of thy youth." I believe it's very important that we accept Christ at an early age. That way, we do not waste a lot of time trying to find out what our purpose in life is. We see Jesus at the age of twelve being about the ways of God.

In Luke 4: 1-14, we see the devil tempting Jesus. Jesus was getting ready to step into his public ministry at age thirty and the devil was going to see if he could destroy his ministry before it was started. We see Jesus once again exercising his ability to stay focused. Jesus had his mind on the things of God. His flesh may have been weak, but his spirit was willing. The Bible says he was full of the Holy Ghost and we see he hit the devil with the word of God. And he walked away victorious.

In the mean while his disciples prayed him, saying, Master, eat. But he said unto them, I have meat to eat that ye know not of. Therefore said the disciples one to another, Hath any man brought him ought to eat? Jesus saith unto them, My meat is to do the will of him that sent me, and to finish his work.

John 4:31-34

Here we see the disciples coming to Jesus and telling him to eat. Jesus said, "I have meat to eat that you know not of." The disciples thought he was talking about physical food, but Jesus was talking about his assignment. He was talking about his purpose and the destiny that God ordained for his life. Jesus' mind was constantly on the plan that God had ordained for his life. He was saying it was more important than physical food. Not to say that food is not important, but we see Jesus staying focused and reminding his disciples that they too should be exercising their ability to stay focused. And also reminding us that we should stay focused on God's plan for our lives.

I want to show you one more example of Jesus exercising his ability to stay focused. In Matthew 26, it talks about the Last Supper. Judas has betrayed Jesus and they have come to take Him away. One of the disciples pulls out his sword and cuts off the ear of one of the high priests. Jesus tells him to put away his sword. In verse 53, He shows once again how He exercised His ability to stay focused. He said thinkest thou that I cannot now pray to My Father, and He shall presently give more than twelve legions of angels. Jesus is saying I do not need you to defend me. He says in verse 54, "But how then shall the scriptures be fulfilled, that thus it must be?" In other words, if I do not exercise my ability to stay focused, than my assignment will not be completed. Think about when they were beating, slapping, spitting on Him, and putting a crown of thorns on His head, through all of that, He stayed focused. And He stayed focused all the way to the cross. He said, if I do not stay focused, Ralph Phifer is going to hell. Your name falls here also. My friend, you have the ability to stay focused but it's up to you to exercise that ability. Not only do we have Jesus to look at, but there were also men and women of God who exercised their ability to stay focused. Look at Nehemiah who rebuilt the walls of Jerusalem, despite great opposition and temptation. What about Noah who finished the ark? It took over one hundred years to complete. Think about all the ridicule he went through being laughed at and talked about, but he maintained his focus and so you can.

Decide to Finish

We have all heard the statement, "It's not how you start it is how you finish that counts." Many people have started things and never finished them. It's easy to start something, but it takes something to finish it. How many people started out walking with God but are no longer walking with God? How many times have you started a diet and did not finish it? Have you started reading a book and never finished it? What about the garage you started cleaning two years ago? What about that degree you said you were going to go back to school and complete? Not only should we start something, but we must have a finishing mentality.

In the mean while his disciples prayed him, saying, Master, eat. But he said unto them, I have meat to eat that ye know not of. Therefore said the disciples one to another, Hath any man brought him ought to eat? Jesus saith unto them, My meat is to do the will of him that sent me, and to finish his work.

John 4:31-34

74

We see the disciples coming to Jesus saying master eat. They were referring to Physical food. Jesus replied I have food to eat that you know not of. The disciples thought that someone had given him food to eat. But Jesus was not talking about physical food. He was talking about the assignment that God had given him. In other words, he was saying my meat, my purpose, my assignment, my reason for existing is to do the will of Him that sent me and to FINISH His work. Not only was Jesus' mind on his assignment, but it was on finishing his assignment. When you set out to do something great, you have to see the end before you see the beginning. The end result is what will keep you pressing toward the end. Because when you are reaching toward your goal, there will be many opportunities to quit. There are going to be times in your life when you will feel like it's not worth it. But you must press on because the reward is greater that the suffering and pain you have to go through

Being confident of this very thing, that he which hath begun a good work in you will perform it until the day of Jesus Christ

Philippians 1:6

The scripture is saying that the good work God started I you, he will see it finished in you. Let's look at this scripture a little closer. In other words God has created us to do good work. Ephesians 2:10 declares that. We have an assignment. God will help us see to it that our assignment is complete. But we have to cooperate. We have to keep our focus on that assignment. We must be persistent. We must persevere. When things get tough, we must not quit, and give up. There are things that will come and try to get us distracted. It's like when a runner is running a race. He will get tired. He will look to see who's around him. If he's winning, he will strategize how to keep the lead. Should he speed up, should he slow down? When he feels like quitting, he remembers all the hard work he put into training. But he keeps his eyes on the prize. So the scripture is saying, as long as we do our part, God will see to it that we finish out our race. The Apostle Paul said in Philippians 3:14, "I pressed toward the mark for the prize of the high calling of God in Christ Jesus." The key is to keep pressing.

And Jesus said unto him, No man, having put his hand to the plough, and looking back, is fit for the kingdom of God.

Luke 9:62

If you want to complete your race, keep your hand on the plough, and do not look back. In other words, keep your mind and your focus on the assignment that God has given you, regardless of what comes up. If you take care of God's business, God will take care of your business. It's easy to begin, but it takes something to finish.

For, lo, thou shalt conceive, and bear a son; and no razor shall come on his head: for the child shall be a Nazarite unto God from the womb: and he shall begin to deliver Israel out of the hand of the Philistines

Judges 13:5

This scripture is talking about Samson. The angel of the Lord had appeared unto Samson's parents and told them what they should do, concerning the life of Samson. I want you to pay close attention to one sentence that the angel stated, "He shall begin to deliver Israel out of the hand of the Philistines." Now I want you to pay close attention to one word in that phrase and that word is begin. Remember we are talking about being a finisher. Samson is one of the most memorable people in the history of the world, unfortunately not in a good light. He is remembered for his great feats of strength. He is also in what we call the hall of faith, which is in the book of Hebrews 11; but he is most remembered for his downfall with Delilah. God raised Samson up to deliver the children of Israel, out of the hands of the Philistines. We remember the words of the angel of the Lord. He will BEGIN, to deliver the children of Israel out of the hands of the Philistines. When we study the life of Samson, we see a man who did not exercise his ability to stay focused. And because he did not, he did not finish his assignment. Samson was sidetracked; he had gotten distracted. He let the pleasures of this world, pull him away from God's plan for his life. He put his hand to the plough, but he looked back. Samson did not destroy the Philistines, he was only a thorn in their side. If Samson had done what God had called him to do, David would have never had to face Goliath. The Philistines would have been destroyed. David finished what Samson was supposed to have finished. I can only imagine what Samson's life would have been like if he had stayed focused and finished what God had called him to do.

I have fought a good fight, I have finished my course, I have kept the faith.

II Timothy 4:7

The Apostle Paul was coming to the end of his life and he is saying I have finished my assignment. What an awesome statement! That's a statement I desire to make one day. Don't you want to make that statement also? If we look at the life of Paul, we see great tribulations, trials, temptations, heartaches, and pain. He had many distractions, nearly stoned to death, friends walking away, and death threats; he kept his hands on the plough and pressed ahead. You and I must press ahead if we are going to finish the assignment that God has given us. Be a finisher.

Chapter 10

Watch your words

In the beginning God created the heavens and the earth. The earth was without form and void, and darkness was over the face of the deep. And the spirit of God was hovering over the face of the waters. And God said let there be light and there was.

Genesis 1:1-3

The Bible tells us that when God created the heavens and the earth, it was without form and void. There was darkness upon the face of the earth, but God spoke to that situation and said, "Let there be light," and there was light. The same goes for you. You are going to have to speak to your situation because words have power. Your words are like seeds. When you speak they go out into the atmosphere and they produce the harvest that you speak. I heard something that was astonishing. I've heard scientists have a device that can detect words that were spoken in the atmosphere over one hundred years ago. Think about that. Your words could be out in the atmosphere.

There's an old saying that says "Sticks and stones may break my bones, but words will never hurt me." That's one of the biggest lies that has ever been told. Words can destroy you. I worked with a young lady who was a wonderful Christian. We would always talk about the things of God. One day she told me that she desired to interview for another job. I encouraged her to do so. So we prayed about it and she decided to do it. The next time she came to work, I asked her how the interview went, and she said she did not go. I asked her why not? She said she went to the interview but when she got out of her car, she remembered the words that her mother had spoken to her when she was a little girl. Her mother had said, that she would never amount to anything. She told her she wished she had never been born and how dumb and stupid she was. Words can hurt you.

Death and life are in the power of the tongue

Proverbs 18:21

I believe this scripture is talking figuratively and literally. Have you ever had an idea or a dream, you shared it with someone and they just shot it down with their words? And it just killed the situation. Let's reverse the situation. Have you ever shared an idea or dream with someone, but you heard words of encouragement that filled the atmosphere and you felt like you could do anything? We can't always control what someone else says, but we can control what we say.

Have faith in God whosoever shall say unto this mountain be thou removed and be thou cast into the sea and shall not doubt in his heart but shall believe those things which he saith thy shall come to pass and they shall have whatsoever he saith

Mark 11:22-23

Jesus said if you do not doubt and believe, you will have what you say. I said what you say. I heard a story of a woman, who was in the hospital with cancer. She had been healed but the cancer had come back. The pastor and members of the congregation, would visit and pray with her. She would say all the right things when people would come. After some time, she passed away. The pastor and the congregation were surprised. Not long after she passed, a lady approached the pastor and told him she was there in the midnight hours when no else was around; and she said the lady would constantly say, "I know I am going to die, I am not going to be healed, this time I do not feel that the prayers are working, I know I am going to die, I wish I was dead, or I feel like dying." She would plant a seed and then pluck it up with her words. I am not saying she died due to her confession alone, but I believe it played a part.

By faith we understand that the worlds were framed by the word of God.

Hebrew 11:3

God framed the world by his words and he will frame our world by our words. The word of God tells us that out of the abundance of the heart, the mouth speaks. So what is in you will come out of you, so it is very important what we put in us. If you put the word of God in you, the word of God will come out of you. If you put junk in you, then junk will come out of you. So choose to put the word of God in you and that's what will come out of you. It's your decision. I like what Charles Capps said, he said, "The word of God conceived in human spirit and formed with the tongue and spoken out the mouth releases the ability of God." That's powerful. You words are powerful. Psalm 19:14 says, "Let the words of my mouth and the meditation of my heart be acceptable in thy sight Oh lord my strength and my redeemer." This scripture tells me that my words can be pleasing or displeasing to God. It's my choice. I choose what I say. You can choose to speak these things which are pleasing to God or displeasing. The choice is yours.

No Fear

You were not born to fear. There are 365 times in the Bible you will find "fear not," one for each day of the year. Fear, is one of the biggest weapons of the devil. He knows if he can get you into fear, he can stop you from fulfilling your destiny. Fear will keep you, from doing what God tells you to do. Fear will keep you from stepping out, when God says step out. God told King Saul to go and destroy Am'alek, to destroy all they had and spare nothing: not man, woman, infant, suckling, ox, sheep, camel, or ass. However, Saul disobeyed. He brought back the king alive; he kept sheep and oxen. When Samuel confronted him about what he had done, this is what Saul said:

And Saul said unto Samuel, I have sinned for I have transgressed the commandment of the Lord, and thy words; Because I feared the people and obeyed their voice.

I Samuel 15:24

Because he feared the people, Saul disobeyed the word of the Lord. One of my friends who is a pastor, had major problems in his church. The church eventually split up. I was talking to him one day and he told me one of the biggest mistakes he made, was he sought to please the people. He feared what they thought instead of what God wanted him to do. When Adam and Eve sinned against God in the garden, the Lord came to them in the garden. He asked Adam, where art thou? He wasn't talking about where he was physically. God knew where he was physically. God was talking about where he stood.

And the Lord God called unto Adam, and said unto him, where art thou? And he said, I heard thy voice in the garden, and I was afraid, because I was naked; and I hid myself.

Genesis 3:9-10

Adam said he was afraid because he was naked. He wasn't afraid because he was naked, it was for the reason that now he had to face the responsibility of his sin. He did not want to be responsible for his sin, so he played the blame game. He blamed God and Eve blamed the serpent. If Adam had stood up and had taken responsibility for his actions, I believe things would have been totally different. But fear kept him from confessing his sin. Many people are walking around today with all kinds of fears. Fearing their bills won't be paid, fearing they will lose their job, fearing safety for their kids, fearing the economy, fearing death, fearing the dark, fearing what the devil's doing, fearing what's under the bed, fearing your past, fearing future. If the devil can get you to act in fear, he's got you. I look at the devil like a bully. If he can take your lunch money, he will. But if you stand up to him, he'll back down. Remember when the devil attacked Job? Job made this statement.

For the thing which I greatly feared is come upon me, and that which I was afraid of is come unto me.

Job 3:25

Job was operating in fear. I do not believe the things that happened to Job were a result of him acting in fear. I do believe, however, it was a factor. Fear is an open door to the devil. Remember the devil is a liar. Whatever he's telling you, just believe the opposite. I would rather believe what God says than what the devil says. Most of the things people fear never happen. I heard the word fear stands for False Evidence Appearing Real. If you are going to be all that God has called you to be, you must overcome fear. Peter denied the Lord three times because of Fear. When he saw what happened to Jesus, he probably thought the same thing would happen to him. We know that he went onto become a great man of God and was killed for his Strong Faith. But at that time fear got the best of him. Why else would he deny the Lord? You must confront your fears and take them head on. The Bible said, David ran toward Goliath. Everyone else was in fear. But David had spent time with the Lord and his faith was built up. He was not trusting in his ability, but the ability of the Lord. We must trust in the Lord and not let fear have a place in us. Many people have missed the will of God for their lives because they allowed fear to get the best of them. Do not be one of those people. You can overcome fear.

I started lifting weights when I was 14 years old. I started Power Lifting when I was 24 years old. James was my workout partner and we were starting to get serious about power lifting. Some people in the gym and around the area would tell me and James that the strongest man in the world lived in town. We did not believe it. We said, why would the strongest man in the world live in Durham, North Carolina? We continued to hear stories everywhere we went. The barber shop, the grocery store, the bank, and so on. Then the day finally came. James and I were working out one afternoon and he walked through the door 6 feet 6inches 420lbs world record holder O.D. Wilson. He was the most massive human being I had ever seen in my life. James and I watched his workout that day. One day I was working out by myself and O.D. walked in. I was squatting and he began to observe me. He came over and said, "You have a lot of power but you do not know how to harness it." At that time, the most I had ever squatted was about 650 lbs. O.D. began to instruct me on some things. He introduced me to knee wraps, squat suits, and squat shoes. The most important words he spoke to me were, "You must never fear the weight, if you do, you will never reach your full potential." We became good friends and workout partners also. Within a year and a half, I was squatting 860lbs. James also made tremendous gains. Fear will stop you from reaching your full potential. O.D. taught me not to fear the weight.

For God has not given us the spirit of fear, but of power of love and of a sound mind.

II Timothy 1:7

Coming out of the comfort zone

Now the Lord had said unto Abram, get thee out of thy country, and from thy kindred, and from thy father's house, unto a land I will show thee.

Genesis 12:1

If you are going to be all God has called you to be, you are sometimes going to have to come out of what I call, the comfort zone. What is the comfort zone? The comfort zone is a place where you have become comfortable. It's a place that you are familiar with, a place that you feel safe and secure, a place that you might not want to leave. You may have grown up there, started a family there, have a good job, established friends there, started a church there, or built a business there. I am sure this is probably what Abram was going through. Then all of the sudden the Lord said get up, leave your country, your relatives, and your father's house; go to a land that I will show you. And I will make of you a great nation. I will bless them that bless you and curse them that curse you. And in thee shall all families of the earth be blessed. I do not believe this was an easy decision for Abram. I heard a saying that goes, sometimes you have to give up something good in order to have something great. I believe Abram saw the bigger picture. He believed the words God spoke to him. And today we see the effect of his decision. He went down in history as one of the greatest men ever. He is known as the father of our faith. He trusted God till the end.

Look at the story of Ruth. She chose to follow Naomi. She left her home of Moab, a place where she had been all of her life. But she believed something better was in store for her, and it was. She was faithful to Naomi her mother-in-law. Naomi's husband and Ruth's husband died where they were in Moab. Naomi decided to return to Bethlehem. Naomi tried to get Ruth and her other daughter-in-law to stay in Moab. The other daughter-in-law stayed, but Ruth followed Naomi.

And Naomi had a kinsman of her husband's, a mighty man of wealth, of the family of Elimelech; and his name was Boaz.

Ruth 2:1

Boaz fell in love with Ruth and showed her great favor. Ruth asked Boaz why she had found favor in his eyes. Listen carefully to what he said.

And Boaz answered and said unto her. It hath fully been showed me, all that thou hast done unto thy mother-in-law since the death of thine husband; and how thou hast left thy father and thy mother, and the land of thy nativity, and art come unto a people which thou knewest not here to fore. The Lord recompence thy work, and a full reward be given thee of the Lord God of Israel under whose wings thou art come to trust.

Ruth 2:11-12

What an awesome statement because she chose to come out of her comfort zone and put her trust in God, she reaped a great reward. She ended up marrying Boaz and was in the lineage of Jesus our Lord. Read the book of Ruth, it will bless you.

I think about Eva Lefever, a missionary who attended the same church as I did. The church supported her financially and prayerfully. She is about seventy years old. She's over in the jungle of Africa preaching the gospel to natives. This woman left her home here in America, to do what God had called her to do. Her life has been in danger and we have had to pray for her protection several times. I met her at a luncheon while she was visiting the states and told her what a great job she was doing. Talk about coming out of the comfort zone, from a nice house in America to the jungle of Africa. And I do mean the jungles. Some churches and our church as well, brought her a van because the only way of travel she had was by foot and canoe. But just think about the blessings she is receiving and will receive in heaven, leading those natives to Christ. Believe me, it's much more rewarding to come out of the comfort zone, than it is to stay in it. The late Dr. Lester Sumrall tells the story of a man and his wife who were called to the mission field of China. The wife did not want to leave their nice house and lifestyle they had established in America. The man was struggling with the whole thing and eventually gave into his wife's wishes. They both died prematurely. I am not saying God killed them because they did not go to China. Of course not, but you do open up the door for the devil when you are disobedient. I said it before and I say it again, God will not call you to do something and not give you a desire to do it. If He's calling you out of your comfort zone, rest assured he's calling you to higher ground. I did not say it would be easy, but I guarantee it will be rewarding. If you ever intend to do anything great, you are going to have to be willing to launch out. You look at the life of any great person, and at some point in their life they had to step out and take a risk. When I was in college, a teammate of mine had a sign on his door that said, "why not go out on a limb, that's where the fruit is." If you are not willing to go out on a limb, you will never get the fruit; the fruit that God has for you. Moses could have stayed in the house of Pharaoh. I am sure it was very comfortable there. But he, like Abraham, saw the big picture. If God is calling you out of your comfort zone, look at the big picture. In the end you will be glad you did.

Chapter 11

Decide to pay the price

I want to ask you some questions:

What is it that you want from God? What do you want God to do in your life? What do you want to do for God? What price are you willing to pay? How bad do you want what you say you want? To get what you want is going to come with a price tag. Have you ever gone into a store and seen something you like; then you looked at the price tag and said no way? In other words you were saying, I am not willing to pay the price for that item. Are you willing to pay the price to fulfill the assignment God has called you to do?

For which of you, intending to build a tower sitteth not down first and counteth the cost, whether he have sufficient to finish it? Lest haply after he hath laid the foundation, and is not able to finish it, all that behold it begin to mock him, Saying this man began to build and was not able to finish.

Luke 14:28-30

Jesus is saying before you step out, to follow Him and make sure you have counted the cost. I remember when the Lord began dealing with my heart about getting saved. I ran for about three months, when I finally considered giving my life to Christ, I sat down and thought about the price I would have to pay. I thought about the commitment I would have to make. I thought about things, people, and places I would have to give up because they would not be beneficial to my Christian walk. Jesus is telling us everything must come second to Him.

And a certain ruler asked him, saying, Good master what shall I do to inherit eternal life? And Jesus said unto him, Why callest thou me good? None is good save one, that is God. Thou knowest the commandments, Do not commit adultery, Do not kill, Do not steal, Do not bear false witness, Honor thy father and mother. And he said All these have I kept from my youth up. Now when Jesus heard these things. He said unto him. Yet lackest thou one thing; sell all that thou hast, and distribute unto the poor, and thou shalt have treasure in heaven; and come follow me. And when he heard this he was very sorrowful for he was very rich.

Luke 18:18-23

I found it very interesting that when this man came to Jesus, he asked how to receive eternal life. Jesus told him what he needed to do. It seemed at first that eternal life was his main concern. But when it came right down to it, his riches were the most important thing. One thing I believe this man failed to realize, is that following Jesus doesn't mean you will be poor. It meant that riches could not be your main priority.

But seek ye first the kingdom of God and His righteousness; and all these things shall be added unto you.

Matthew 6:33

This scripture is saying put the things of God first and all these things shall be added unto you. What things? The houses, cars, and land. Notice that God called them things. They are just things. So many people are concerned about the things and not about God's kingdom. If you take care of God's business, He will take care of your things.

Then Peter began to say unto Him, lo we have left all and have followed Thee. And Jesus answered and said, Verily I say unto you, there is no man that hath left house, or brethren, or sisters, or father, or mother, or wife, or children, or lands, for My sake and the gospel's. But he shall receive a hundred-fold now in this time, houses, and brethren and sisters, and mothers, and children, and lands, with persecutions; and in the world to come eternal life.

Mark 10:28-31

Jesus is saying, there is nothing that you won't give up, that will not be restored to you. And not only restored but a hundred-fold return. But notice what He said in the latter part of this scripture, WITH PERSECUTIONS. In other words there is a price to pay. I'll ask you again, what price are you willing to pay? All too often we look at the people who have achieved great things. But we do not look at the price they had to pay. The trials, tribulations, heartaches, pains, slander, and the discouragement they had to go through, the times they wanted to give up. I heard a lady ask T.D. Jakes if she could have the anointing that he has by laying his hands on her. He said you can't have my anointing without the trials, struggles, pain, tribulations, and heartaches. He was telling her there is more than meets the eye. She just saw him ministering to thousands of people and wanted to be in the limelight. But she did not see the price he paid to get there. Think about Abraham leaving his home to go to a place he knew not of. Think about Ruth following Naomi to a strange land trusting in her God. What about Elisha leaving his home, friends, and family to follow Elijah and fulfill the call of God on his life. The Apostle Paul who was stoned, beaten, deserted, thrown in prison, and shipwrecked. And of course the one who paid the ultimate price, our Lord and Savior Jesus Christ. Yes my friend, there is a price to pay. Now you have to decide, are you willing to pay that price?

Dare to dream

When we pastored a church, there was a young lady named Ami who attended. As we got to know Ami, we found out her husband was the pilot for NASCAR driver Matt Kenseth. When I met her husband, he told me how he had become a pilot. It was a fascinating story. Elwood grew up in the Bahamas. He lived on Crooked Island, which was 30 miles long and 7 miles wide. Elwood had an interest in flying. He would see the planes flying by and dreamed of being a pilot. Elwood's father passed away when he was six years old, but he remembered his father telling him, that whatever he dreamed he could accomplish. Elwood's mother had a desire for him to be a chef. He actually received a scholarship for culinary school. Elwood wanted to be a pilot. He had found a school to attend. Family and friends had saved up $20,000 dollars in order for him to attend school. Elwood had paid his tuition and was ready for school. Then the unthinkable happened. A few weeks before he was to attend school the school filed bankruptcy. His $20,000

91

was lost. Elwood was devastated but not defeated. Elwood had some friends that lived in Florida. One day while visiting them he saw an aviation school. He walked in the school and began to tell them his story. They informed him of the tuition and what it would take for him to enroll in the school. Determined more than ever Elwood began to devise a plan. So what Elwood did was during the winter months, he would work in the Bahamas as a diver and in the summer, he would attend school in Florida. Elwood was focused on one thing and one thing only, that was becoming a pilot. He did not go on a date for two years. He did not go out and hang with the boys. He was totally focused on his dream. He knew he had to be on top of his game. His grades were always in the 90's. In three and a half years he received his pilot's license. He said he realized he had his pilot's license and did not have his driver's license. He began to fly many race teams. Matt Kenseth was on one of these teams. When Matt decided to buy his own plane he chose Elwood to be his pilot. He has been Matt's pilot for the last eleven years. Elwood is totally living his dream.

3 Keys to Elwood fulfilling his dream

1. **He took ownership of his dream**- Elwood's dream was his dream. It was what was in his heart. Even through his mother wanting him to be a chef, he was determined to fulfill what was in his heart. When you are trying to fulfill someone else's dream when things get tough, it can be easy to abandon those dreams. But if it's what's in your heart, you will not surrender when times get tough

2. **He did not allow hardship to destroy him**- My friend if you are going to reach your dreams, you must understand that you will have to overcome difficult times. How easy would it have been for Elwood to give up and quit after that twenty

thousand dollars was lost? That was a devastating blow. If you are going to be an overcomer, than you must overcome some things. His dream was so strong, that he continued to press forward even in the face of adversity. When you look at the life of great people, you will see that they had to overcome setbacks and the same is true with you. It's part of the process.

3. **He stayed focused until the task was finished**-when Elwood was in school, he was totally focused. He did not go on a date for two years, he did not hang out with the boys, he put his mind to the task, and did not look back. You will have to give up something good to get something great. You have the ability to stay focused. You just have to make the decision to do it.

Decide to renew your mind

The mind is a battlefield. It is where the war will be won or lost. I believe that's the number one place the devil attacks. Every action begins with a thought. When a person accepts Christ as their Lord and Savior, the first thing they need to do is to renew their minds, with the things of God. I got saved when I was twenty-seven years old. That was twenty-seven years of thinking like the world. Now I had to start thinking like God.

For as he thinketh in his heart so is he; Eat and drink, saith he to thee; but his heart is not with thee.

Proverbs 23:7

What you think about, you will become. And what you allow in your mind, you will think on. So it's very important that you guard your mind. The mind is a very powerful tool. I have heard of a study where a scientist put a fish in a tank with minnows. The fish loved to eat minnows, but the scientist put a glass plate between the fish and minnows. The fish banged his head against the glass, trying to get the minnows. After a few days the scientist pulled out the glass that was separating the fish and the minnows. The fish and the minnows swam in the same tank, but the fish did not even attempt to eat the minnows. Why? Because mentally he was convinced that he couldn't get to the minnows. The devil will put all kinds of thoughts in your mind, but you can't let him convince you they are true. He has the ability to put thoughts in your head, but you do not have to think on what he puts in there. He does not know what you are thinking; he puts a thought in your mind and if you act on it, he knows he's got you. The devil is a liar, so you know that anything he tells you, just believe the opposite.

Finally brethren whatsoever things are true, whatsoever things are honest, whatsoever things are just, whatsoever things are pure, whatsoever things are lovely, whatsoever things are of good report; if there be any virtues, and if there be any praise think on these things.

Philippians 4:8

Paul is telling us what we should think about. When I got saved, I had to change what I was putting in my mind. I changed the television shows I watched. I changed the music I was listening to. I changed the people I hung around. I had to change some of the material I was reading. I had to replace those things with the things of God, watching Godly shows, what little there is, listening to gospel music, fellowshipping with likeminded Christians, reading the Bible, and other Christian books. Understand that this is not an overnight process. Remember I was twenty-seven when I got saved. Twenty-seven years is not going to go away overnight. When I was at the University of North Carolina at Chapel Hill, our football coach brought in a running specialist. He was going to help us improve our running style. He worked us out twice a day for one week telling us to lift our knees, keep our elbows in tight, to keep our head straight, and so on. When he left, the coach continued to emphasize the specialist's techniques. But I noticed something in some of our games and practices. Guys were running the way they had run before the specialist came. We were 19, 20, 21 year-old guys who had been running that way since we were kids. One week of two a day practices will not change that. But if we continued to be aware of how we were running, and the coaches kept emphasizing it, we could make progress. The same way with renewing your mind. Make the effort and be aware of what's going into your mind.

And be not conformed to this world; but be ye transformed by the renewing of your mind, that ye may prove what is that good, and acceptable, and perfect, will of God.

Romans 12:2

Do not let this world conform you into its ways or should I say mold you. That's what conform means, molding you like a piece of clay. And that is exactly what will happen, if you do not renew your mind. But be transformed like a caterpillar into a butterfly, by renewing your mind with the things of God.

When the unclean spirit is gone out of a man, he walkath through dry places, seeking rest, and findeth none. Then he saith, I will return into my house from whence I came out; and when he is come, he findeth empty, swept, and garnished. Then goeth he and taketh with himself seven other spirits more wicked than himself and they enter in and dwell there; and

the last state of that man is worse than the first. Even so shall it be also unto this wicked generation.

Matthew 12:43-45

You can't afford to keep your mind empty. You must fill it up with the things of God. If you do not replace those old things with new things, the old things will come back worse than before.

Let this mind be in you which was also in Christ Jesus.

Philippians 2:5

Thou wilt keep him in perfect peace, whose mind is stayed on Thee; because he trusteth in thee.

Isaiah 26:3

Decide to be an overcomer

You were born to overcome. You were born to win. You were born to be successful. There is nothing that you will face in your life that you are not equipped to handle.

There hath no temptation taken you but such as is common to man; but God is faithful, who will not suffer you to be tempted above that ye are able; but will with the temptation also make a way to escape, that ye may be able to bear it.

I Corinthians 10:13

The first part of that scripture says, there is no temptation taken you but such is common to man. In other words, there is nothing that you have faced, are facing, or will face that someone else hasn't faced also. So many times people think they are going through something that no one else has been through. You are sadly mistaken. There are people who have faced greater trials than you and they overcame it. You were built for life. The second part of that

96

scripture says GOD IS FAITHFUL who will not suffer you to be tempted above that ye are able. In other words, God will not allow you to go through something that you can't handle. Why would He do that? If He created you to overcome, why would He put you in a situation where you could not overcome? The last part of that scripture says that God will make a way of escape. In other words, He has an answer to your problem. I think about Joyce Meyers, who is one of the greatest ministers of the gospel in the world. I listen to her tapes series entitled, "Trophies of Grace", which was her life story. You talk about someone who had overcome a tragic childhood, a failed marriage, and a ton of problems. What a testimony! You talk about someone who had an opportunity to pack it in. But look at her today. With God on her side and her will to win, she overcame incredible odds. Kenneth Hagin on his deathbed, rose above death to become one of the greatest men of influence in the world today. Oral Roberts dying of tuberculosis, tragic deaths in his family, name slandered, overcame it all to become a great man of influence. I could go on and on about people who overcame great odds. You can probably think of many yourself. I think about the life of King David. A man who experienced many setbacks in his life, but became the greatest king Israel ever knew.

One of the greatest traits about David, was that he came back strong after a setback. He did not sit around crying why me? He got up and took charge of the situation. Let's look at some of the setbacks that happened to David. First of all, he was rejected by his father. When Samuel the prophet went to Jesse's house to anoint the new king, David wasn't even present. He was tending to the sheep. After Samuel had gone through all his brothers, he said do you have any more sons? Jesse said yes, the youngest David, he's out with the sheep. He did not think enough of David to invite him to the event. His brothers did not care too much for him as well. After he killed Goliath, King

Saul became jealous and tried to kill him. He was on the run from Saul. He slept with Uriah's wife Bathsheba and she became pregnant; and to cover up the situation, he had Uriah killed. If he had been in battle where he was supposed to be, this wouldn't have happened. His son Absalom tried to steal the kingdom from him. David disobeyed the Lord and as a result, 70,000 men died. With all of these setbacks, David is still one of the greatest men in the history of the world. Life is full of trouble. You will have problems, trials, tribulations, defeats, and temptations; how you handle them is what counts. You will get knocked down, but will you get back up? Another example of a great overcomer is Joseph. He was sold into slavery by his brothers, lied on, thrown into prison, forgotten about when in prison, but he rose to become the second highest man in power behind Pharaoh. I want to give you three things you must do to be an overcomer.

The first thing is to meditate on the word of God daily and apply the word to your life.

This book of the law shall not depart out of the mouth but thou shalt meditate therein day and night, that thou mayest observe to do according to all that is written therein; for then thou shalt make thy way prosperous, and thou shalt have good success.

Joshua 1:8

Second, have a consistent prayer life.

And He spoke a parable unto them to this end, that men ought always pray, and not to faint.

Luke 18:1

Thirdly, have faith.

Then came the disciples to Jesus apart and said, why could not we cast him out? And Jesus said unto them because of your unbelief; for verily I say unto you if ye have faith as a grain of mustard, ye shall say unto this mountain remove hence to yonder place; and it shall remove; and nothing shall be impossible to you.

Matthew 17:20

Chapter 12

You Can Bounce Back

"I can do all things through Christ which strengthens me."

Philippians 4:13

I believe that whatever a person has been through, regardless of circumstances or situation, they can bounce back. People have made decisions in life that have been devastating. Unfortunately, some have never recovered. There have been some that were serving God, and just because another member in the church hurt their feelings, they left the church and never returned. There are some people who have made bad financial decisions, and then committed suicide. There are people who were told as a child that they were worthless and would never amount to anything; they allowed this to affect them for the rest of their lives, and never regained their confidence. This person might be 60 or 70 years old now, and may have missed the will of God for their life. Some people are in mental institutions, possessing various gifts and talents, but because of one or more difficult situations, or an instance in their life that overwhelmed them, they will never reach their full potential. There are many people who have been through divorces and never bounced back.

People have chosen the wrong mate and never bounced back. These are all very sad situations, because with God's help we can bounce back from anything. I realize that we all have different levels of tolerances, but the Bible states that *nothing* is impossible to them that believe. We all have within us a measure of faith. We can all be victorious. It is up to us to tap into what God has placed on the inside of us.

"There hath no temptation taken you but such as is common to man; but God is faithful, who will not suffer you to be tempted above that ye are able: but, will with the temptation also make a way to escape that ye may be able to bear it."
                                                     1 Corinthians 10:13

       The first part of this scripture is saying that you are not going through anything that someone else has not already been through. All too often we think we are the only people enduring a particular, painful situation. There are people who are enduring these types of situations or worse. They are being victorious in their situations. They are making it through with flying colors. There is an old saying that says, "There is nothing wrong with getting knocked down, as long as you don't stay down." My friend, as long as you are on this earth you will face trials, tests and challenges. You are going to have to decide to fight. The Apostle Paul said, "Fight the good fight of faith." You will never achieve anything great in life without putting up a fight. We have an enemy out there that will stop at nothing to try and destroy us. Many of us make the mistake of thinking God is the one who tempts us. It is not of God. Why would He tempt us? For He is God, and He knows where our faith rests. The devil is the one who tries our faith. When we say we are going to stand on the promises of God, the devil is the one who brings a negative situation to try and test our faith, to see if we will stand or waiver. If we stand up and say we believe in divine healing, the devil may try to cause pain in our bodies to determine if we truly believe God's promises. If we pledge our tithes and offerings, and believe God for an increase in finances, a financial hardship may come in our lives to test our faith. If you believe God to deliver that unsaved spouse or loved one, their behavior may become worse. Don't be mistaken - every time you stand on the Word of God, it doesn't mean you'll experience the opposite of that Word to test and try your faith. But recognize that the enemy is going **to and fro seeking about whom he may devour**. The devil is the prince and power of the air. Don't be fooled into thinking that the devil is all-powerful and he can do what he wants, because he can't. As a child of God we have dominion; the devil can't touch you. Greater is He that is in you than he that is in the world. God is greater. The devil has so many of us fooled into thinking he can do whatever he wants. This is not so.

The second part of this scripture states that God is faithful, who will not allow us to be tempted above that we are able to bear. If God allows you to be tempted, you can handle it. You may not think that you can, but if God allowed it, you are able to overcome any situation. Not just to go through it and suffer through it, but to be victorious. Why is it that two people can be involved in the same set of circumstances, and one comes through it, and the other does not? Because one made the decision to trust God and take Him at His Word, and the other did not. I am sorry, but there are no excuses.

We cannot blame our environment, or where we were born. Many people come from ghettos and projects as well as other negative conditions, and make it through. We cannot blame our racial or cultural differences for our lack of achievement. People from all sorts of ethnic backgrounds have overcome. The government can't be made to blame. Our parents are not to blame. We can bounce back. How many times have you seen a sports team come back from a huge deficit and be victorious, even though it seemed impossible? What about the 1996 World Series? The Yankees were down 2 games to none against the Braves. The Yankees came back to win the World Series. Time and time again, we have witnessed people overcome, even with their backs against the wall. My brothers and sisters in Christ, we must be born again. With Jesus on our side, there is nothing we cannot accomplish, nothing we cannot endure. We hear people quoting scriptures like "I am the head, and not the tail," "No weapon formed against me shall prosper," and "My God shall supply all my need." These scriptures only apply to the person who has accepted Jesus Christ as their Lord and Savior.

The second step is to have the right attitude. Many of us are failing in life because of a negative attitude. We must practice a positive attitude. The way we face a particular situation will determine our outcome. If you wake up in the morning and say, "This is going to be a terrible day," then it probably will be. If you want your circumstances to change then your attitude must change. We must be watchful of our words. Proverbs 18:21 tell us death and life are in the power of the tongue. We must make positive confessions. We must surround ourselves with like-minded believers. The old saying, "Birds of a feather flock together", holds true. If you want to soar like an eagle, you can't run with turkeys. Associate with people who have the same goals and directions as you. We must also forgive others who may have hurt us. Many of us are walking around with bitterness in our hearts toward others. You only hurt yourself with this type of anger. Some are even sick in their physical bodies because of un-forgiveness in their heart. Un-forgiveness can cause you to be a prisoner to sin. You must forgive in order to bounce back. Regardless of what has happened in the past, my brothers and sisters in Christ, we can and must bounce back. Remember it is a decision.

A Decision for Christ

"Behold, I stand at the door, and knock: if any man hear my voice, and open the door, I will come into him, and sup with him and he with me."
Revelation 3:20

The most important decision you will make in life is to accept Jesus Christ as your Lord and Savior. But, as I stated before, this is your choice. God gives us a free will, and from that will, we make decisions. These decisions we make determine our destiny. Brothers and sisters, you will spend eternity either in heaven, or in hell. There are no if, ands, or buts about it. Once you take your last breath on earth, you will pass into eternity. Where you will end up is determined by the decision you made while you were here on earth. God will not force us to do anything, because that would go against our own will to choose. God will not force His will upon us, even if it means us going to hell. God doesn't choose to send anybody to hell. You send yourself by rejecting Jesus Christ as your Lord and Savior. People are falsely thinking that there are many ways to get to heaven. My Bible tells me there is only one way. Jesus said:

"I am the way, the truth and the life. No man comes to the Father but by me."
John 14:6

I heard someone say that some people are destined for hell, and some are destined for heaven. What kind of God would God be if He said, "This person is going to hell, and this person is going to heaven?" Where we spend eternity is based on our decision for Jesus Christ. It is God's desire that no man should perish, but all should come to the knowledge of God - I Timothy 2:4. I love Billy Graham's magazine and radio program, entitled the <u>HOUR OF DECISION</u>. That is exactly what God gives us - the right to make our own decisions.

For years I wondered about the scripture, "Many are called, few are chosen." Then one day I was watching Kenneth Copeland's broadcast, and he was talking about this scripture. He stated, "God calls everyone to get saved, but the ones who decide to accept salvation are the ones who are chosen." Matthew 22:1-14 explains how everyone is called, but not everyone will accept the call. It is God's will that everyone be saved. But of course, this is not what will happen.

"Who will have all men to be saved, and to come unto the knowledge of the truth?"
I Timothy 2:4

Accepting Jesus Christ as our Lord and Savior is a must decision. Not only does God give us a choice, but He also advises us on the decision to make.

"I call heaven and earth to record this day against you, that I have set before you life and death; blessing and cursing: THEREFORE CHOOSE LIFE, that both thou and thou seed may live."
Deuteronomy 30:19

God gives us a choice and He tells us what we should choose. God is for us; He is not against us. He loves us and cares for us; He wants the best for us. My friend, if you die and go to hell, you will have to buck, fight, kick, and scream against the love of God. Nobody will be able to stand before God on judgment day, and say, "You gave me a bum deal!" To get to hell, you would have to climb over the Cross, disregard the Blood of Jesus, and reject the preaching of the Gospel. In addition, you would have to overcome the prayers of loved ones, resist the prompting of the Holy Spirit, ignore the convictions of your own conscience, and that is just to name a few of the opportunities God lines up along your path to reveal His love to you. Jesus Christ is knocking at your heart; it is your choice to decide whether or not to let Him in. He will not knock the door down. Brothers and sisters, choose life. If you have not accepted Jesus Christ as your Lord and Savior and you would like to, simply pray this prayer:

Lord Jesus, I am a sinner. But I ask You to come into my heart. Wash me in your blood. Forgive me of my sins. I turn from my wicked ways and accept You as my Lord and Savior. Satan I no longer belong to you, I belong to God. Thank you, Jesus, for saving me. Amen.

If you sincerely prayed this prayer, I want to welcome you to the family of God. You need to find yourself a church home that preaches and teaches the Word of God, read your Bible, and pray daily, fellowship with Christian brothers and sisters, and let the Holy Spirit guide you.

Chapter 13

8 Steps to Making a Good Decision

Step #1

<u>Know the Word of God</u>

The first step in making a good decision is to see what the Word of God says about the situation.

"So shall my word be that goeth forth out of my mouth: it shall not return unto me void, but it shall accomplish that which I please, and it shall prosper in the thing whereto I sent it."

Isaiah 55:11

It doesn't matter what you feel, or what someone else says or thinks about a situation; the only thing that truly matters is what the Word of God *states;* only God's position on the subject has authority. I have stated this many times - "be ye not unequally yoked." Whether or not the person may be attractive, or financially wealthy, is not important; if the person does not know Jesus Christ as his personal Lord and Savior, he or she is not the mate for you. There are so many Christians who have married non-Christians, and because of this, have experienced hell here on earth with regards to their marriage. What makes a person think that they can change another person if God hasn't changed them? I have even heard a few pastors say that they told some of their members not to marry their intended mate because they were unequally yoked, yet the member would try to convince the pastor how nice the person was. But, the Word of God clearly states **"be ye not unequally yoked!"** Finally, the member tells the pastor, "But I have needs." The Word of God instructs us, **"be ye not unequally yoked!"** Unfortunately, most of us know what the Word of God says, but we want to follow our own hearts and minds anyway. Some people justify this behavior because they *want* to marry the person; and they *choose* to marry despite God's instruction, and months or years later, end up in divorce.

In Luke chapter 4, the devil tries to tempt Jesus. However, if you notice, Jesus defeated the devil with the Word of God. Jesus didn't argue with the devil, or debate with him. Jesus simply stated what the Word of God said. God's Word has a solution to every problem that arises. If we are having problems with finances, the Word of God instructs us to *bring all the tithes to the storehouse.* If we are experiencing sickness in our bodies, go to the Word; children rebelling - go to the Word; problems in our marriages - go to the Word. Many of us experience difficulties because we want <u>instant</u> resolution. We live in a fast-paced society, and therefore we are used to commanding fast food, fast banking, and instant food preparation using microwaves. *People want things, and they want them now; they demand them instantly.* We must stand on the Word of God. If God **says** it, then it will come to pass. It may not be when you *want* it, but it will be right on time! Great men and women of faith have stood on the Word of God until God performed what He said He would do.

Step #2

Pray

"Be careful for nothing; but in everything by prayer and supplication with thanksgiving let your request be made known unto God."
Philippians 4:6

The second step you need to take before making a decision is to pray. Talk to God and seek His face. He will reveal to you what He wants you to do. The devil despises prayer, especially when we pray in our heavenly language. The devil does not know what you are saying when you pray in tongues. It is a tremendous weapon against the devil. If you are planning to make a major decision, like moving to a different city, a job change, or marriage, there should be quality time spent in prayer. I am convinced that many Christians don't have a prayer life. Prayer is the key that unlocks the door. We will never be successful in what we aspire to do, unless we seek God through prayer. Jesus said in Luke 18:1, "Men ought always to pray and faint not." Jesus often spent time alone praying to God. Prayer gives us power. After Jesus had been off praying to God, He came to His disciples *walking on the water.*

God desires to spend time listening and talking to His children. We often say, "God knows what our desires are," and He does, but He still desires fellowship with us. If you have children, you want to know what their concerns are, you want them to talk to you, and share things with you. We need to be specific with God when we have a prayer request. So many of us pray incorrectly. When we don't get the results we were seeking, we think that God didn't answer our prayers. We must realize that the way we pray affects our answered, or unanswered prayers. Many of us just pray to God in general terms:

God bless my family; God bless my job; God bless the food; God I desire a mate; or God I desire a new house. General prayers get general results. Some of us get faster results to our prayers than others. This is because those who understand how to pray tend to be more effective. I can leave my house in Mooresville, NC, travel Interstate 77 South, and arrive in Charlotte in about 25 minutes. Or, I can leave my house, travel on Interstate 77 North, go to Statesville, then take Interstate 77 South, come through Davidson, Cornelius, and about an hour later arrive in Charlotte. Both routes will get me to Charlotte, but the first route will get me there much sooner. If we know how to pray correctly, then we can obtain results faster. We must also pray in line with the Word of God. We need to study prayer so that we will be more effective in our prayer lives. Prayer is very important, but improper prayer can be wasted time and emotion. If you have not been receiving answers to your prayers, you need to go back and study how to pray. We must never make decisions without taking time to pray.

Step #3

Seek Godly Counsel

"Blessed is the man that walketh not in the counsel of the ungodly."

Psalm 1:1

It is very important when we are making a decision that we seek godly counsel. This godly counsel comes from men and women of notable reputation, who have influenced our lives and spiritual growth in a positive manner. These men and women of God can consist of your pastor, a spiritual mentor or teacher, a mature Christian, and other people of strong spiritual influence. I have talked to many people in ministry that have given me nuggets I will treasure for life. Many times these men and women of God can help us to avoid pitfalls in our lives by sharing their own mistakes and experiences. John Wesley, one of the greatest preachers ever, believed that God had called him to be single like the apostle Paul. However, some of his friends felt that he needed to get married, and talked him into finding a wife, and marrying her. John was not a very large man, but his wife was. She ended up physically abusing him, and attempted to destroy his ministry. John Wesley was the founder of the Methodist Church. The reason they called it the Methodist Church was because the word Methodist comes from the word method. John Wesley would utilize certain methods on a regular basis for prayer, preaching, witnessing, and teaching. One of John's methods was to never make a decision without consulting four of his godly friends, but for some unknown reason he didn't consult them before he married this woman. The marriage was a disaster, and resulted in a divorce. The lesson is that we should never make a major decision without seeking godly counsel.

I know a young lady who was getting married. Her pastor told her they needed to come in for counseling. They did not want counseling, and got married anyhow. (Before I finish the story, I want to say something about counseling. If you do not want to be counseled, I think there is a problem. In my opinion, people who don't want counseling have something to hide. Why wouldn't you want to get godly advice? Godly counsel can help prevent you from pitfalls that could have been avoided. I wouldn't dream of getting married, or making any major decision without good godly counsel.) Now back to my story. Even though many friends had advised her not to marry, she ignored their advice. The marriage was hell on earth and still is. She has suffered tremendously. The point I am trying to make is that she refused to accept godly counsel.

first from her pastor and then her friends. She made a decision and it cost her. In my opinion, Godly counsel is a must when it comes to making quality decisions. I am not saying you should listen to everything everyone tells you, but godly counsel is a key principle in decision-making.

"Where no counsel is the people fall, but in a multitude of counselors there is safety."
Proverbs 11:14

Step #4

Control Your Emotions

I once heard a saying that goes, "Emotions can make a fool out of you." Many people have made bad decisions based on their emotions. Your soul consists of your mind, will, and emotions. I said earlier that our spirit should lead us. I also said that when there is a decision to be made, your soul will cast the deciding vote. The way your soul will vote depends on how much you have renewed your mind with the Word of God (See Chapter 6, Spirit Led Decisions). A decision based on emotions will not last. How many times have we made a decision based on our emotions, and later found out it was not a wise decision. You may have gone into a store and seen something you liked, and purchased it. But later after you got home and thought about it, you realized you really couldn't afford it. Some people have gotten married because they got emotionally involved with the person, only to find out later that they made a big mistake. When we are faced with a decision, we must think things out clearly. In Chapter 3, "Timely Decisions", I talked about times where we must act right away. However, this won't be all the time. Most of the time we need to sit down and put things in their proper perspective. I don't want to sound like emotions are terrible, because they are not. Emotions are good in some cases. God gave us emotions. If we didn't have them, we would be walking around like robots. I am trying to say that we must not allow our emotions to lead us. Sarah made a decision based on emotion. God had promised her and Abraham a child. Thinking that she could help God, Sarah made an emotional decision. She told Abram to go into her handmaiden, Hagar, to conceive a child. After the child was born there was chaos. It got so bad that Abraham had to have Hagar removed from the camp, at Sarah's request. If God has promised you something, it will come to pass. Remember, don't be anxious for anything. Control your emotions, and let your spirit lead you.

Step #5

Count the Cost

"For which of you, intending to build a tower, sitteth not down first, and counteth the cost, whether he have *sufficient* to finish it?"
Luke 14:28

One important step in making a good decision is to consider the cost. I believe if people just took a moment to consider the cost of certain decisions, we would have people making better choices. The crime rate would probably decrease significantly if the perpetrator considered the cost of his or her actions first. If the criminal were to contemplate going to prison, being locked up without any freedom, unable to come and go as they pleased, away from friends and family, they in all likelihood would choose not to commit the crime. What about people engaging in sex outside of marriage? If they considered the fact that they might conceive a child, or that they may have to forfeit plans to attend school, or that they may contract a sexually transmitted disease, or that as a young athlete they may have to resign from sports to work one or two jobs to make ends meet, the person could definitely arrive at a better choice for themselves. If a person who chooses to cheat on their spouse knew beforehand that they would be caught, the embarrassment they would face, the hurt and emotional damage to the spouse, and maybe even children, and the possibility of divorce should be reason enough to reconsider such an irresponsible choice.

I read a story once where a woman had stolen over $800,000 from the bank where she worked for over a ten-year period. When she was finally caught, all of her possessions, as well as her husband's possessions, were taken from them. The house, cars, boats, jewelry, stocks, bonds, furniture, etc. In addition, she received imprisonment. What a price to pay! If she had only considered the cost before taking such an action.

I enjoy lifting weights. I have been lifting ever since I was 14 years old. When I was 25, I seriously considered a career in power lifting. I knew that many of the people I would be competing against were using steroids. I had to consider whether or not I would take steroids as well to remain competitive. My decision was to simply sit down and weigh the cost. I had to consider whether or not it would be worth the physical risk of putting chemicals into my body that could possibly cause serious health problems long-term, as well as the criminal aspects of using an illegal drug. All this for temporal gain. I decided that temporary success and financial gain were not worth the risk of ruining my future, or possibly destroying the rest of my life. We all must stop to consider the cost of our choices, and what affect they will have in our life as well as the lives of others. Ask yourself if the consequences are worth it. Is not accepting Jesus worth an eternity in hell? Nothing on this earth is worth risking hell for. You may enjoy sin for a time, but the end result will be unbearable. Even if you are one of those who don't believe in hell, are you willing to take the chance that it doesn't exist? One of the most horrifying realities of hell is the loneliness. You are eternally separated from God. Some might ask, "What if I do go to hell?" All of my friends will probably be there too, and we can have a big party. Your friends may indeed be there, but I promise you it will be anything but a party. The only way you will recognize them is from their screams. It will be so dark and desolate that you won't be able to see your own hand, even if you put it right in front of your face. Hell is not a destination that you experience for a little while and then it is over. Hell is forever! Whatever is keeping you from accepting Jesus Christ as your personal Lord and Savior is not worth losing your soul for an eternity. I encourage you to count the cost.

Step #6

<u>Learn from Others' Mistakes</u>

Another step toward making a good decision is to simply learn from others. The old saying, "You have to experience something before you can learn something," is totally untrue. Experience is not the best teacher. Why would I go through a hardship someone has already been through, when I see it has destroyed his or her life? If drugs ruined a person's life, then I don't need to experiment with drugs myself to determine if they would destroy my life as well. If alcohol destroyed a person's life, then I don't need to test alcohol to determine whether or not it will destroy my life. It is very important that parents share their failures as well as their successes with their children. So many parents say, "I don't want my children to know about my past." If we share our past with them, we can keep them from making the same mistakes we made. I have spoken to several pastors who have given me insight with regards to life in the ministry. They have shared their successes as well as their failures with me. I will take heed so I don't end up making the same mistakes. Since they have chosen to share their experiences and wisdom with me, there are choices that I may have made in error if I had not gotten godly counsel. One reason people try things after they have been told not to is because they think they are going to be the exception to the rule. They believe they are smarter, and that the situation will be different for them. They have the attitude that no matter what happened to the other person, it will not be the same for them. Another reason people don't learn from other people's experiences is that they feel that no one can tell them what to do. If you do not have a teachable spirit, you will find yourself making mistakes you could have avoided. I don't know everything, and I don't mind letting everyone know that I don't know everything. Anything I can learn that will benefit me, I want to learn. We don't know everything, but we can all learn together. Keep an open mind; don't be so closed-minded that no one can tell you anything. You can learn from the mistakes of others.

Step #7

Use Common Sense

The seventh step toward making a good decision is using plain old common sense. God gave us a brain, and He expects us to use it. We know when we are faced with a decision, whether it is right or wrong. Solomon was the wisest man that ever lived aside from Jesus Christ, but even he made bad decisions. You can have wisdom, and still make wrong decisions. Wisdom is the ability to take understanding and knowledge, and apply it to the everyday principles of life. If you know what is right but you didn't choose to do it, then you didn't use what you learned properly. If you surround yourself with people whom you know are heading for trouble, and you continue to hang around them, common sense should tell you, "You are heading for trouble." How many times have we done something that we knew was wrong, yet we did it anyway? This was not using good common sense. We have the ability to make good decisions, and common sense falls in that category. God has given us many gifts, and common sense is one of those gifts. USE IT.

Step #8

Never Make a Decision When You Are Tired or Under Stress

It is very important that when you make a decision you are well rested. The late Dr. Lester Sumrall said he never made a major decision after 2:00 o'clock in the afternoon. He said your mind is tired after making decisions and dealing with the affairs of life all day. I believe you are at your best mentally and physically after a good night's sleep. When you are tired, you are not as sharp as you would normally be. If we make decisions under pressure or stress, we are sure to make bad decisions. If someone tells you that you have to make a decision today, tell him or her to forget it. Car salesmen are known for this tactic. They say that if you don't buy this car today, the deal will no longer be available. Parents sometimes make a decision when they are tired, or under stress, only to later realize they made a bad decision. Remember, Sarah made a bad decision under stress. Relax, evaluate the situation, and never make a decision when you are under stress.

I can do all things through Christ who strengthens me.

Phillipines 4:13

Whatsoever is born of God overcometh the world and this is the victory that overcometh the world even our faith.

I John 5:4

For we are his workmanship created in Christ Jesus unto good works which God hath before ordained that we should walk in them.

Ephesians 2:10

Ye are of God, little children, and have overcome them because greater is He that is in you then he that is in the world.

I John 4:4

Nay, in all these things we are more than conquerors through Him that loved us.

Romans 8:37

About the Author

Ralph Phifer is a native Mooresville, NC. He attended the University of North Carolina at Chapel Hill on a football scholarship. He graduated in 1988 with a BA degree in sociology. He attended School of Life Bible School, in Sand Springs Oklahoma, where he graduated in 2000. He has been a lead pastor, a youth pastor, and ministered in prisons. He is a dynamic speaker who now has a healing ministry. He has a lovely wife Bridget, and two beautiful children Christopher and Destini.

<u>Notes</u>

<u>Notes</u>

Notes

Made in the USA
Middletown, DE
10 September 2024

60687224R10073